ANY BITCH CAN TOSS IT

AND WE MEAN THIS IN
A GOOD WAY!

<u>B</u>abe <u>I</u>n <u>T</u>otal <u>C</u>ontrol of <u>H</u>erself

"I'm a light eater.
When it gets light, I start eating."
Tommy John

ISBN #1-57166-516-1

Printed by
Jumbo Jack's Cookbooks
Audubon, IA

TABLE OF CONTENTS

Soups

BEEFY TORTILLA SOUP

1 lb. lean ground beef or turkey
1-14 oz. can diced tomatoes, undrained
1-4 oz. can diced green chili peppers
2-15 oz. cans kidney beans
1 C. water
1 pkg. taco seasoning mix
1 pkg. Hidden Valley Ranch dressing mix
1 C. frozen corn
Tortilla chips
Shredded cheddar cheese
Sour cream

Brown the meat and remove the excess fat. In a large pot or crock-pot, add the beef and the rest of the ingredients. Cooking on the stove, simmer for 45 minutes to 1 hour. If you are cooking in a crock-pot, cook on low all day. When ready to serve, crush the chips and place in the bottom of the bowl. Sprinkle on the cheese and top with a dollop of sour cream. Serves 4.

BARLEY BEEF SOUP

1 lb. hamburger
1 onion, chopped
2-10 3/4 oz. cans condensed beef broth
2 cans water
1 C. carrots, diced
1 C. celery, diced
1 C. turnips, diced
1/2 C. barley
3/4 t. salt
1/8 t. pepper
1 bay leaf

Brown the hamburger and onion. Drain off the fat. Add all the rest of the ingredients and bring to a boil. Reduce heat and simmer for an hour. Serves 6.

EIGHT-CAN SOUP

Carolyn Boehm, Audubon, Ia.

1 lb. lean ground beef, browned

1-10 3/4 oz. can condensed tomato soup, undiluted

1-10.5 oz. can condensed vegetable soup, undiluted

1-15 oz. can chili with beans

1-15 oz. can chili without beans

1-15 oz. can mixed vegetables, undrained

1-14.5 oz. can diced tomatoes, undrained

1-10 oz. can diced tomatoes with green chili peppers, undrained

1-15 oz. can whole kernel corn, undrained

Add all the ingredients to a 6-quart, no smaller, crock-pot and stir until completely mixed together. Do not drain liquid. Do not add additional liquid either. Simply heat on high for 30 to 45 minutes, or until mixture starts to bubble, then turn to low. It is ready to serve. To make it taste better, let it cook on low for 3 to 4 hours.

I don't know what your problem is.....but I bet it's hard to pronounce.

TURKEY AND BARLEY SOUP

6 C. water
1/4 C. barley
1 C. onion, chopped
1/2 C. celery, chopped
1 T. chicken bouillon
  granules

1/2 lb. turkey breast,
  boned, skinned and cut
  into bite-size pieces
1 T. sour cream and
  butter-flavored sprinkles
1/2 t. lemon pepper
  seasoning

Bring the water to a boil and add the barley. Reduce the heat and simmer for 15 minutes, stirring occasionally. Add the onions, celery and bouillon granules and continue cooking for 20 minutes. Add the remaining ingredients and cook for 20 more minutes. Serves 4.

Never go to bed angry.....stay up and plot your revenge!

TEX-MEX TURKEY SOUP

1 T. olive oil
1/2 C. minced onion
3 cloves garlic, minced
2 t. chili powder
1/2 t. cumin
1/2 t. oregano
4 C. water
1-10.75 oz. can condensed
  tomato soup
1-28 oz. can diced
  tomatoes

1 C. salsa
4 C. shredded cooked
  turkey
1 T. dried parsley
3 chicken bouillon cubes
1-14 oz. can black beans,
  rinsed and drained
2 C. frozen corn
1/2 C. sour cream
1/4 C. chopped fresh
  cilantro

TOPPINGS:
6 C. corn tortilla chips
3/4 C. chopped green onion
1 C. shredded Cheddar
  cheese

1/2 C. chopped fresh
  cilantro
1/2 C. sour cream

Heat the olive oil in a large saucepan over mediu heat.
Add the onions and cook until soft. Add the garlic,
chili powder, cumin and oregano, and cook, stirring,
for 1 minute. Stir in the water, tomato soup, tomatoes,
salsa, turkey, parsley and bouillon cubes. Bring to a
boil. Reduce heat and simmer 5 minutes. Add the beans,
corn, sour cream and cilantro. Simmer for 30 minutes.
Serve with the toppings. Serves 6.

CHICKEN TACO SOUP

1 onion, chopped
1-16 oz. can chili beans
1-15 oz. can black beans
1-15 oz. can whole kernel
  corn, drained
1-8 oz. can tomato sauce
1-12 oz. can beer
2-10 oz. cans diced
  tomatoes with green
  chilies

1-1/25 oz. pkg. taco
  seasoning
3 whole skinless, boneless
  chicken breasts
Cheddar cheese, shredded
Sour cream
Crushed tortilla chips

Add the first 7 ingredients in a slow cooker. Add the taco seasoning and stir to blend well. Lay chicken breasts on top of the mixture, pressing down slightly until just covered by the ingredients. Set on low heat, and cook for 5 hours. Remove the chicken breasts and shred. Stir back into the pot and cook for 2 more hours. Serve topped with the cheese, sour cream and chips. Serves 8.

If you have something to say, raise your hand and place it over your mouth.

CHICKEN SALSA SOUP

Judy Wilkers

1 whole chicken
1-16 oz. jar salsa
1 can corn, drained
1 can black beans, drained
  and rinsed

Sour cream
Shredded cheese
Fritos or baked tortilla
  chips

Place the chicken in a crock-pot and pour the salsa over. Cook until the chicken falls off the bones. Debone chicken and cut up into bite-sized pieces. The salsa forms the broth, but it will be a thick stew. Add the corn and black beans. Spoon it out into bowls and add the sour cream, cheese and chips on top.

SIX-CAN CHICKEN TORTILLA SOUP

1-15 oz. can whole kernel
  corn, drained
1-14.5 oz. can chicken
  broth
1-10 oz. can chunk chicken

1-15 oz. can black beans
1-10 can diced tomatoes
  with green chilies,
  drained

TOPPINGS:
Shredded cheddar cheese
Tortilla strips

Sour cream

Place all ingredients in a large pot. Simmer over medium heat until heated. Place toppings on top. Serves 6.

LOBSTER BISQUE

1 onion, chopped fine
1/2 C. butter
3/4 C. flour
2 C. chicken broth
1/4 t. white pepper

1-11 oz. can frozen
 lobster meat
3/4 C. sherry
3 C. cream
2 T. tomato paste

Sauté the onions in the butter for 2 to 3 minutes. With a whisk, stir in the flour until smooth. Add the broth and pepper. Cook, stirring constantly, until thickened. Add the lobster meat and cook 20 minutes. Blend in sherry, cream and tomato pate. Serves 6.

SHRIMP AND ARTICHOKE SOUP

1 T. butter
1 lb. peeled medium shrimp
1 bunch green onions,
 chopped
6 C. canned fat-free
 chicken broth

3 C. thinly sliced peeled
 potatoes
1-14 oz. can artichoke
 hearts, drained and
 halved
Salt and pepper to taste
1/2 C. cream

Sauté the shrimp and green onions in the butter, about 5 minute. Set aside. In a pot, bring the broth to a boil. Add the potatoes, artichokes, salt and pepper. Return to a boil and continue boiling for 10 minutes. Transfer to a food processor and purée. Return to the pot and add the shrimp mixture and cream. Stir to heat. Serves 6.

FAST CRAB BISQUE

1-10 oz. pkg. frozen mixed
 vegetables
1-10.75 oz. can condensed
 cheddar cheese soup
1-10.75 oz. can condensed
 cream of mushroom soup
1 qt. half-and-half

3 T. sherry
1 t. Worcestershire sauce
1-6 oz. can crabmeat,
 drained, flaked and
 cartilage removed
1 tomato, seed and chopped
1 T. butter

Cook the frozen vegetables according to the package
directions and drain. In a saucepan, place the soups,
half-and-half, sherry and Worcestershire sauce. Mix
well and bring to a simmer, stirring frequently. Stir
in the vegetables, crabmeat, tomato and butter. Heat to
serving temperature. Serves 6.

CRAB SOUP

1/2 C. butter, melted
1/4 C. flour
4 C. milk
2 T. finely chopped onions

2 t. chicken base
1/8 t. pepper
2 T. chopped parsley
1 lb. crabmeat

Mix the butter and flour with a whisk. Cook for 3
minutes, then stir in the milk, onion, chicken base,
pepper and parsley. Reduce the heat and cook until
thick. Stir in crabmeat and heat. Serves 4.

CRAB SOUP

Patty Daniels, Tideline Gallery,
Rehobath Beach, De.

2 shallots, finely chopped	2 C. half-and-half
2 T. butter	2 C. heavy cream
1 clove garlic, finely chopped	Parsley, chopped, for garnish
1 t. crab spice	1 T. cornstarch
1 lb. lump crabmeat	1/4 C. cold water

Sauté shallots and garlic in butter until transparent, approximately 3 to 5 minutes. Add half-and-half, heavy cream and crab spice. Simmer 10 minutes. Gently add crabmeat and bring to a slow boil. Mix cornstarch and water, slowly adding to the soup. Stir until desired thickness. Remove from the heat and spoon into bowls. Sprinkle with parsley and a pinch of crab spice.

QUICK VEGETABLE SOUP

1 onion, chopped	1 T. Worcestershire sauce
1 t. minced garlic	1 small bay leaf
1-16 oz. can tomato purée	1 C. sliced carrots
4 C. water	1-10 oz. pkg. frozen corn
1/2 t. salt	1-10 oz. pkg. frozen green peas
1/2 t. pepper	
1 T. light brown sugar	1/3 C. rice

In a large pot, sauté the onions and garlic until done. Add the rest of the ingredients, except the peas and rice. Bring to a boil and simmer for about 20 minutes. Add the peas and rice, cover, and simmer about 45 minutes longer. Remove the bay leaf before serving. Serves 6.

BASIL VEGGIE SOUP

1 t. butter
1 onion, chopped
1 celery stalk, sliced
1 carrot, sliced
1 potato, peeled and cubed
2 tomatoes, diced
2 C. vegetable broth
1 C. tomato sauce

1 t. dried basil
1 C. cauliflower tops
2 zucchini, sliced
1 C. white cabbage, chopped
Salt and pepper to taste
1/2 C. parmesan cheese, grated

Melt the butter in a large soup pot. Add the onion, celery and carrots, cooking until vegetables are soft. Add the potatoes, tomatoes, broth, tomato sauce and basil. Bring to a boil and simmer for 15 minutes. Add the remaining vegetables and simmer for 15 to 20 minutes. Add the salt and pepper. Sprinkle the cheese on top. Serves 6.

BLACK BEAN AND SALSA SOUP

2-15 oz. cans black beans, drained and rinsed
1 1/2 C. vegetable broth
1 C. chunky salsa

1 t. ground cumin
4 T. sour cream
2 T. thinly-sliced green onion

In a food processor or blender, combine beans, broth, salsa and cumin. Blend until fairly smooth. Heat the mixture in a saucepan over medium heat. Top with a dollop of sour cream and the green onions. Serves 4.

THREE-BEAN SOUP

1 C. dried red kidney
  beans
1 C. dried Great Northern
  beans
1 C. dried black beans
1 T. butter
1 C. chopped onion
1 green bell pepper,
  seeded and chopped
1 T. minced garlic

1 1/2 C. diced peeled
  carrots
8 C. water
2-10 oz. cans diced
  tomatoes and green
  chilies, drained
1 1/2 t. dried oregano
1 t. dried thyme
2 bay leaves
Salt and pepper to taste

Soak the beans overnight. Drain and rinse. In a large
pot, melt the butter and sauté the onion, green pepper,
garlic and carrots over medium-high heat for 3 to 5
minutes. Add the remaining ingredients, except the salt
and pepper. Bring to a boil. Cover and reduce the heat
and cook for 2 hours. Remove the bay leaf before
serving. Season with the salt and pepper. Serves 10.

*I'm going south for the winter.....actually some parts
of me are headed there already.*

TORTELLINI, WHITE BEAN AND SPINACH SOUP

Grace Qualls, Lafayette, La.

3 garlic cloves, minced
1 large onion, chopped
1 medium red bell pepper, chopped
1 t. dried Italian seasoning
1 T. olive oil
2-14.5 oz. cans chicken broth
1-16 oz. can navy beans, rinsed and drained

1-14.5 oz. can chopped tomatoes, undrained
1-14 oz. can artichoke hearts, drained
1-9 oz. pkg. refrigerator cheese-filled tortellini
2 c. coarsely chopped fresh spinach
1 C. shredded parmesan cheese

Sauté first 4 ingredients in hot oil in a large Dutch oven over medium-high heat. Add broth and next 3 ingredients. Bring to a boil, reduce heat and simmer 2 minutes. Add tortellini and spinach and simmer 5 minutes. Sprinkle with the cheese. Makes 1 1/2 quarts.

"If you can keep your head, when all about you are losing theirs and blaming it on you."
                                        -Rudyard Kepling

PASTA FAGIOLI

Suzy Garvey, Treasure Seekers, Charlotte, NC.

1/2 lb. small shell
  macaroni, cooked al denté
1 lb. Great Northern beans
4 qt. water
2 t. tomato paste
2 t. salt

1/2 t. basil
1/2 t. oregano
2 t. granulated garlic
1 C. olive oil
Parmesan cheese
Pepper to taste

Cook beans in water for 15 minutes, boiling hard. Add the rest of the ingredients, except the macaroni, and keep boiling until beans are done. Add the pasta. Soup should be 30% macaroni and 70% soup. Just before serving, add the cheese and pepper to taste. Serves 8.

SPLIT PEA SOUP

2 C. dried split peas
5 slices turkey bacon, cut
  into pieces
1 onion, chopped
1/2 C. celery, chopped
4 C. chicken broth

1 bay leaf
2 C. carrots, sliced
1 potato, peeled and diced
Salt and pepper to taste
1/2 t. dried thyme

Soak the peas in water to cover overnight. In a soup pot, sauté the bacon, onion and celery until tender. Add the peas with the water and remaining ingredients. Bring to a boil, lower heat and cook, covered, for 2 hours. Stir occasionally. Remove the bay leaf before serving. Serves 6.

CREAM OF SPINACH SOUP

1/2 lb. fresh mushrooms, sliced
1 T. butter
1 onion, chopped
2-10 3/4 oz. cans cream of mushroom soup

1-14 1/2 oz. can chicken broth
2-10 oz. pkg. frozen chopped spinach, cooked according to pkg. directions, drained well
Salt and pepper to taste

Sauté the mushrooms and onion in the butter until tender. Add the soup, chicken broth, spinach, salt and pepper, stirring until thoroughly heated. Transfer to a blender or food processor and purée. Serves 8.

EGG DROP SOUP

6 C. chicken broth
3 T. cornstarch in
 2 T. water
1 T. soy sauce

1/2 t. sugar
2 eggs, slightly beaten
Salt and pepper to taste
2 scallions, diced

Bring broth to a boil. Combine cornstarch mixture with the soy sauce and sugar. Add the salt and pepper. Slowly stir into the broth. Heat and continue stirring until thick and clear. Remove from the heat. Gradually add the eggs using a wide pronged fork. Stir with the fork to separate the eggs as they cook. Garnish with the scallions. Serves 4.

SQUASH SOUP

1 T. cumin seeds
1 onion, cut in chunks
1 lb. butternut squash,
  cut in chunks

1 clove garlic
3 C. chicken broth
1/2 C. heavy cream
Salt and pepper to taste

Place the cumin seeds in a soup pot over medium heat.
When the seeds begin to snap in the pot, remove from
the heat. Add the onions and squash to the pot. Peel
the clove of the garlic and add to the pot. Add the
broth, salt and pepper and bring to a boil. Reduce the
heat and simmer for 30 minutes, stirring occasionally.
Add the cream and blend with a hand blender until
smooth. Serves 3.

SQUASH SOUP II

1 acorn squash, cut into
  1/4's, do not peel
1/2 C. dried white beans
2 stalks celery, chopped
1 C. onion, chopped

3 cloves garlic, minced
Vegetable bouillon, enough
  for 2 C. liquid broth
1/8 t. pepper

Soak the beans overnight. Rinse beans and put in a
large pot with 3 cups water. Add the celery, onion,
garlic and bouillon and bring to a boil. Turn down to
simmer. Simmer for 1 hour. Fill another large pot with
water ad bring to a boil. Place the squash in the water
and boil for 15 minutes. Remove the squash and set
aside to cool. Scoop the inside of the squash and place
in a blender. Purée; add to the bean mixture. Add the
pepper and serve.

SANTA FE SQUASH SOUP

1 T. vegetable oil
1/3 C. chopped onion
1-14.5 oz. can chicken
  broth
1 C. diced zucchini
1 C. diced yellow squash

1 C. frozen corn
1-4 oz. can diced green
  chilies
1 C. milk
1/2 C. diced cheddar
  cheese

Heat the oil in a saucepan. Add the onion and cook until tender. Add the broth, zucchini, squash, corn and chilies and bring to a boil. Cover and reduce heat to low; cook for 5 minutes, or until squash is tender. Add the milk and heat just until hot. Stir in cheese. Serves 5.

"I'm allergic to food. Every time I eat it breaks out into fat."

-Jennifer Greene Duncan

BROCCOLI CHEESE SOUP

2-10 oz. pkg. frozen
  chopped broccoli
3 1/2 C. chicken broth
30 fresh mushrooms, sliced
1 C. celery, finely
  chopped
1/2 C. green onion,
  chopped
2 T. finely chopped fresh
  parsley

2 T. butter
2 t. garlic powder
1/2 t. cracked pepper
1/2 t. pepper
1 1/2 C. grated cheddar
  cheese
1/2 C. sour cream
1/2 t. Tabasco sauce

Cook the broccoli according to package directions. Drain. Purée in blender with 1 1/2 cups chicken broth. In a pan, simmer puréed broccoli with remaining chicken broth over medium heat. In a skillet, sauté the vegetables in the butter until onions are transparent. Add the garlic powder and pepper. Add the puréed broccoli. Cover and cook over low heat for 30 minutes. Stir in cheese and sour cream. Season with the Tabasco sauce. Serves 6.

A balanced diet is a cookie in each hand.

BROCCOLI SOUP

1/4 C. onion, chopped
1 T. butter
2 C. milk
1-8 oz. pkg. cream cheese,
  diced

3/4 lb. processed cheese
  spread, diced
1-10 oz. pkg. frozen
  chopped broccoli
1/4 t. nutmeg
1/8 t. pepper

Sauté the onion in the butter until tender. Add the milk and cream cheese and stir over medium heat until the cheese is melted, stirring constantly. Stir in the processed cheese, broccoli, nutmeg and pepper. Heat. Serves 8.

CREAM OF ASPARAGUS SOUP

1 1/2 lb. asparagus
1 1/2 C. chopped onions
6 T. butter
6 T. flour
2 c. chicken broth

4 C. milk
1/2 t. dill weed
1 t. salt
1/2 t. white pepper
2 T. soy sauce

Cut off and discard the tough bottoms of the asparagus. Cut off the tips and set aside. Coarsely chop the stalks. Melt the butter in a skillet over medium-high heat and add the chopped stalks and onions. Cook for 10 minutes, until onions are transparent. Sprinkle the asparagus mixture with the flour and continue to stir over low heat for 8 minutes. Slowly add the chicken broth, stirring constantly. Cool slightly. In a blender, add the mixture and purée. In a soup pot, add the milk, dill weed, salt, white pepper, soy sauce, asparagus tips and purée and heat gently, but do not boil. Serves 4.

WILD RICE AND MUSHROOM SOUP

1-6 oz. box long grain and
  wild rice
1 T. butter
1 onion, chopped
1 lb. sliced mushrooms
1/2 C. chopped green bell
  pepper

1/3 C. flour
4 C. canned fat-free
  chicken broth
1-12 oz. can evaporated
  skimmed milk
Salt and pepper to taste

Cook rice according to package directions. Set aside.
Sauté the onion, mushrooms and green peppers in the
melted butter until tender. Add the flour, stirring.
Gradually stir in the broth and heat until boiling. Add
the milk, rice, salt and pepper. Serves 8.

CREAM OF MUSHROOM SOUP

1 1/2 C. vegetable broth
1 onion, chopped
1 celery stalk, chopped
3/4 lb. mushrooms, sliced
1 T. fresh parsley,
  chopped
1/4 t. nutmeg

2 T. butter
1 1/2 T. flour
1/4 t. salt
1/4 t. white pepper
1 C. milk, you can use
  skim milk
1 1/2 T. sherry

Add the first 6 ingredients to a soup pot and bring to
a boil. Reduce heat and cover for 5 minutes. Place half
of the mixture into a blender and process until smooth.
Pour into a bowl and repeat the other half. Set aside.
In the same pot, melt the butter over medium heat. Stir
in the flour, salt and pepper. Add the milk. Cook and
stir until mixture is thickened and bubbly. Add the
blended vegetables and sherry. Stir until heated.
Serves 4.

CORN CHOWDER

1 stick butter
2 potatoes, diced
2 celery stalks, chopped
1 onion, chopped
4 T. flour
2 t. paprika

1 can chicken broth
1-20 oz. can corn
2 pt. half-and-half
1 1/2 t. salt
Red pepper to taste

Cook the potatoes, celery and onions in the butter.
Stir in paprika and half of the flour. Stir in broth,
over medium heat, stirring for 5 minutes. Stir in corn
and half-and-half. Add the salt, pepper and remaining
flour. Cook on low for 20 minutes. Serves 8 to 10.

TUSCANY TOMATO SOUP

1/4 C. olive oil
4 T. butter
4 carrots, peeled and
 finely diced
4 stalks celery, finely
 diced
3 medium onions, finely
 minced

3-28 oz. cans tomatoes
 with juice
1/2 C. finely chopped
 parsley
1/4 C. minced fresh basil
Salt and pepper to taste

Heat the oil and butter in a large pot. Cook the
carrots, celery and onions for about 20 minutes, or
until very tender. Purée the tomatoes in a blender. Add
to the pot and continue cooking over medium heat for 30
minutes longer. Remove from the heat. Stir in the
parsley, basil, salt and pepper. Serves 10.

HASH BROWN POTATO SOUP

1 pkg. frozen hash browns
4 C. chicken broth
1 pkg. seasoning blend
  (mixed bell peppers,
  onions and celery)
Garlic to taste

1 C. sour cream
1/4 C. bacon bits
1 C. cheddar cheese
1 can cream of chicken
  soup

Cook hash browns and seasoning blend in the broth. Add
the remaining ingredients and simmer for 15 minutes.
Add shredded cheese and sliced green onions to the top.
Serves 4.

BAKED POTATO SOUP

1 medium bulb garlic, 1/4-
  inch cut off the top
6 large baking potatoes,
  pierced once with a fork
4 1/2 C. chicken broth

1/2 t. ground pepper
Bacon pieces
Shredded cheddar cheese
Sour cream
Minced scallions

Preheat oven to 400 degrees F. Wrap the whole garlic
bulb tightly in foil. Put garlic and potatoes in the
oven. Bake garlic 45 minutes. Remove and let cool. Cook
the potatoes for 15 more minutes, or until tender.
Unwrap garlic and squeeze pulp from the bulb into a
large pot. Peel 3 of the hot potatoes, add in the pot
with the garlic and mash until nearly smooth. Gradually
stir in the chicken broth and pepper. Cook over medium
heat and cook until hot, stirring occasionally. Cut the
remaining potato into 3/4-inch pieces. Stir into soup
and heat. Serve with the rest of the ingredients placed
on top of the soup.

SWEET POTATO SOUP

2 T. vegetable oil
2 onions, chopped
2 carrots, peeled and
  diced
1 celery stalk, diced
1/2 C. celery leaves,
  chopped

6 c. sweet potatoes,
  peeled and diced
2 bay leaves
1/4 t. dried thyme
1/4 t. nutmeg
1 C. milk
1/2 t. salt
1/8 t. pepper

Heat the oil in a pot and add the onions, carrots and celery. Sauté over low heat until the onions are translucent. Add the celery leaves and sweet potatoes. Add just enough water to cover all but about an inch of the vegetables. Bring to a simmer and stir in the bay leaves, thyme, nutmeg, salt and pepper. Simmer, covered, until the potatoes and vegetables are tender. With a slotted spoon, remove half of the solid ingredients and transfer them to a food processor with about 1/2 cup of the cooking liquid. Purée and return to the pot. Add the milk and simmer for about 15 minutes. Serves 6.

Salad
Dressings

TERRY'S SALAD DRESSING

Terry Saba, Chandler, Az.

2 C. fresh lemon juice
2 C. canola oil (can use part olive oil)
3/4 C. red wine vinegar

5 T. salt
3 large cloves garlic, crushed
8 black peppercorns

Mix together. Does not need to be refrigerated (olive oil congeals when refrigerated). Shake well.

Use on green salads, potato salad, pasta salad or as a marinade.

CAESAR DRESSING

1 C. salad oil
2 cloves garlic, finely chopped
1/2 t. pepper
1/2 t. salt

1 egg
4 T. lemon juice
1/2 C. Parmesan cheese
2 T. Worcestershire sauce

Soak garlic in oil for 30 minutes. Blend all ingredients in a blender for a few seconds.

Did you eat an extra bowl of stupid this morning?

FRENCH DRESSING

1 C. salad oil
5 T. wine vinegar
1 T. sugar
1/2 t. salt

1/2 t. dry mustard
1/2 t. paprika
1 clove garlic, pressed

Mix all the ingredients well, cover and refrigerate.

GREEN GODDESS

2 T. lemon juice
1 C. mayonnaise
1/2 C. light cream
4 T. wine vinegar
1 clove garlic, pressed

1 T. anchovy paste
1 T. parsley flakes
1/2 small onion, grated
1/8 t. pepper
Dash of Tabasco sauce

Combine the first 3 ingredients and mix well. Add remaining ingredients. Cover and refrigerate.

BLUE CHEESE DRESSING

1 C. sour cream
1/4 C. buttermilk
4 oz. blue cheese,
  crumbled
2 t. minced fresh parsley

1 t. Worcestershire sauce
1/2 t. garlic powder
Kosher salt and pepper, to
  taste

Combine all the ingredients and mix well. Cover and refrigerate. Makes 2 cups.

LOW-FAT RANCH DRESSING

3/4 C. buttermilk
2 T. low fat mayonnaise
2 T. nonfat sour cream
1 T. green onion, finely
  chopped
2 t. white vinegar

1 t. dry mustard
1/4 t. dried thyme leaves
2 garlic cloves, finely
  minced
1/2 t. sugar
Salt and pepper to taste

Place all ingredients in a blender and blend until smooth. Cover and refrigerate. Keeps for 1 week. Makes 1 cup.

PARMESAN SALAD DRESSING

1 C. mayonnaise
1 T. lemon juice
1/2 t. garlic powder
1/2 t. onion powder

1/2 t. pepper
1/2 C. Parmesan cheese,
  finely grated
Salt to taste

Mix all the ingredients together. Cover and refrigerate overnight.

Everyone seems normal until you get to know them!

AVOCADO SALAD DRESSING

1 avocado
1 T. lemon juice
1 T. white wine vinegar
2 t. salsa
1 t. Dijon mustard
Salt and pepper to taste

Cut the avocado in half and remove the pit. Peel. Place in a blender with the lemon juice, vinegar, salsa and mustard. Blend until smooth. Season with the salt and pepper. Chill before serving. Serves 4.

BUTTERMILK SALAD DRESSING

1/2 C. low fat buttermilk
1 T. white wine vinegar
1/2 t. sugar
2 t. Dijon mustard
Salt and pepper to taste
3 green onions, thinly sliced
1 clove garlic, minced

Combine ingredients and chill until ready to use. Makes 3/4 cup.

YOGURT SALAD DRESSING

1/2 pt. yogurt
1 t. lemon juice
1/4 t. garlic salt
1/4 t. onion salt
1 dash celery salt

Stir all ingredients and mix well. Cover and refrigerate until ready to use. Makes 1/2 pint.

TOMATO GARLIC DRESSING

2 C. mayonnaise
1 t. lemon juice

1 t. garlic powder
2 tomatoes, cubed

Process in a blender until smooth. Cover and refrigerate. Makes 3 cups.

CRANBERRY VINAIGRETTE

1/2 C. jellied cranberry
  sauce
1/4 C. red wine vinegar

1/4 C. oil
1 T. Dijon mustard

Place all ingredients in a blender and blend until smooth. Refrigerate until ready to serve.

RASPBERRY VINAIGRETTE DRESSING

1 qt. fresh raspberries
1 1/4 C. white vinegar

1 1/2 C. sugar

Place the berries in a jar and pour the vinegar over. Let stand for 6 days, shaking once a day. At the end of the sixth day, strain the mixture to remove the solids and bring the liquid to a boil. Add the sugar and taste for sweetness before adding all the sugar. Boil for 1 minute. Place in a bottle and refrigerate before serving. Serves 24.

HONEY MUSTARD DRESSING

1 1/2 C. real mayonnaise   1/2 C. honey
1/4 C. Grey Poupon mustard

Stir all ingredients in a small bowl. Cover and refrigerate for 1 hour before serving. Serves 12.

THOUSAND ISLAND SALAD DRESSING

1/2 C. mayonnaise   1 t. sugar
1/4 C. ketchup   1 t. chopped pimento
1 T. distilled white   1/2 t. onion salt
  vinegar   Black pepper to taste
2 t. sweet pickle relish

Stir all ingredients in a bowl and mix well. Cover and refrigerate. Makes 1 cup.

FIESTA DRESSING

1-8 oz. ctn. plain yogurt   1 t. ground cumin
3 T. minced onion   1 t. chili powder
1 1/2 T. fresh lime juice   1/4 t. salt
1 clove garlic, minced

Combine all ingredients and mix well. Makes 1 cup.

SUN-DRIED TOMATO AND BASIL VINAIGRETTE

4 sun-dried tomato halves,
  not packed in oil
Boiling water
1/2 C. fat-free reduced-
  sodium chicken broth
2 T. fresh basil, finely
  chopped

2 T. olive oil
2 T. lemon juice
2 T. water
1 clove garlic, minced
1/4 t. salt
1/4 t. pepper

Place tomatoes in a small bowl. Pour the boiling water over the tomatoes just to cover. Let stand 10 minutes. Drain well and chop. In a small jar with a tight fitting lid, combine all ingredients and shake well. Chill until ready to use. Shake before using. Makes 1 cup.

COLESLAW DRESSING

1 1/4 C. mayonnaise
1/3 C. sugar
1/4 C. cider vinegar
1/4 t. celery seed

1/2 t. seasoned salt
1/4 t. pepper
Salt to taste

Combine all ingredients in a jar and shake well. Refrigerate until ready to use.

Eat, drink and re-marry.

CITRUS VINAIGRETTE

1/4 C. balsamic vinegar
3 T. orange juice
2 1/2 T. lime juice
2 T. honey mustard
2 T. olive oil
1 large green onion,
  including top, thinly
  sliced

3 cloves garlic, minced
1/2 t. dried basil
1/2 t. dried oregano
  leaves
1/4 t. salt

Combine in a jar with a tight fitting lid. Refrigerate until serving time. Shake well before using. Makes 2/3 cup.

FRUIT DRESSING

4 egg yolks, well beaten
4 T. tarragon vinegar
1 T. sugar
1 T. butter
1/2 t. salt

1 t. dry mustard, mixed
  with a little water
Dash of red pepper
1 pt. cream, whipped

Cook the first 7 ingredients in a double boiler, stirring constantly, until thick. Cool. Fold in the whipped cream before serving. Add any fruits you would like. Makes 1 1/2 pints.

POPPY SEED SALAD DRESSING

1 1/2 C. sugar
1 T. dry mustard
1 t. salt
2/3 C. cider vinegar

2 C. vegetable oil
2 T. poppy seeds
1/4 C. grated onion

Combine the first 4 ingredients in a blender. Add the oil slowly, blending until thick. Stir in the poppy seeds and grated onions. Store in an airtight container in the refrigerator. Shake before using. Makes 3 cups.

God put me on this earth to accomplish a certain number of things. Right now, I am so far behind I will never die!

Notes

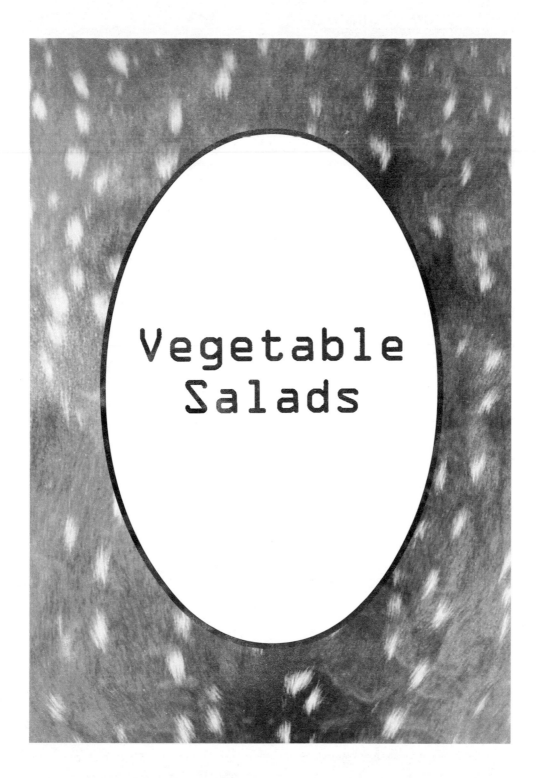

Vegetable
Salads

SPINACH AND GOAT CHEESE SALAD

SALAD:

12 C. baby spinach leaves
1 lb. fresh, creamy goat
  cheese, divided into 8
  equal rounds
1/4 C. olive oil

Salt to taste
White pepper to taste
1/2 C. roasted pecans
2 T. finely chopped fresh
  chives

DRESSING:

1/2 C. balsamic vinegar
2 T. dried cherries
8 dried apricots, cut into
  1/8-inch wide slivers

1 t. creamy Dijon mustard
1 t. honey
1/2 C. olive oil

Put the vinegar in a small saucepan. Heat over medium heat until bubbles begin to appear around its edges. Remove the pan from the heat and add the dried cherries and apricots. Cover and let stand for 10 minutes. Remove the fruit from the pan with a slotted spoon and set aside. With a whisk, stir the mustard and honey in the pan of vinegar until blended. Place over medium low heat, pour the 1/2 cup oil in a thin steady stream and stir continuously. Turn off the heat and return the dried fruit to the pan and cover. Preheat the broiler. Arrange the spinach on individual serving plates. On a shallow baking dish, cover with foil. Place the cheese rounds in the pan. Lightly coat each round with some olive oil. Sprinkle with the salt and pepper. Place under the broiler for 1 to 2 minutes. With a spatula, transfer 2 cheese rounds to each plate of spinach. Drizzle the warm dressing over and garnish with the pecans and chives. Serves 6.

STRAWBERRY AND PECAN SPINACH SALAD

8 oz. fresh spinach, torn
1 1/2 C. sliced
  strawberries

1/2 C. pecan halves,
  lightly toasted
3 oz. goat cheese,
  crumbled

DRESSING:
1/4 C. salad oil
2 T. balsamic vinegar
1 T. + 1 t. sugar
1/4 t. dried tarragon

1/8 t. onion powder
1/8 t. garlic powder
Dash of dry mustard

Toss the first 4 ingredients. Add the rest of the ingredients in a jar with a lid. Shake until well blended. Drizzle over the salad. Serves 6.

POPPY SEED AND STRAWBERRY SPINACH SALAD

1 bunch spinach
10 large strawberries,
  sliced
1/2 C. sugar

1 t. salt
1/3 C. white wine vinegar
1 C. vegetable oil
1 T. poppy seeds

Place the spinach and strawberries in a bowl. Add the sugar, salt, vinegar and oil to a blender. Blend until smooth. Stir in the poppy seeds. Pour over the spinach. Serves 4.

STRAWBERRY SPINACH SALAD

Michael and Peter, Queens Garden,
South Weymouth, Ma.

1 lb. spinach leaves
3 scallions, chopped
2 C. strawberries,
  quartered
1 orange, peeled,
  sectioned and cut
1/4 C. cashews

3 T. honey
1/2 tsp. salt
1/2 tsp. mustard
1/2 tsp. paprika
1/2 C. salad oil
2 T. vinegar

Combine the first 5 ingredients in a bowl and chill for
10 minutes. Mix the rest of the ingredients. Pour over
the salad and serve immediately.

ORANGE AND SPINACH SALAD

4 C. torn fresh spinach
2 oranges, peeled and
  sectioned
3/4 C. sliced fresh
  mushrooms
2 T. salad oil

1 T. lemon juice
1 T. honey
1/4 t. poppy seed
1/8 t. garlic powder
1/4 C. toasted slivered
  almonds

Mix the first 3 ingredients and toss. In a jar, combine
the rest of the ingredients, except the almonds. Cover
and shake well. Pour over the salad and toss. Sprinkle
with the almonds. Serves 4.

CRANBERRY SPINACH SALAD

1 T. butter
3/4 C. slivered almonds
1 lb. spinach, torn into
  bite size pieces
1 C. dried cranberries
2 T. toasted sesame seeds
1 T. poppy seeds

1/2 C. sugar
2 t. minced onion
1/4 t. paprika
1/4 C. white wine vinegar
1/4 C. cider vinegar
1/2 C. vegetable oil

Melt the butter and add the almonds. Cook over medium heat, and stir until lightly toasted. Let cool. In a bowl, add the spinach, almonds and cranberries. Whisk together the rest of the ingredients. Toss with the spinach. Serves 8.

FRESH FIG AND SPINACH SALAD

3 T. rice vinegar
3 T. walnut oil
2 T. snipped fresh mint
1 clove garlic, minced
Salt and pepper to taste
6 C. torn spinach
1/3 C. toasted walnuts,
  chopped

6 fresh figs, quartered
  lengthwise
1 red grapefruit, peeled
  and sliced crosswise
3 oz. fresh goat cheese,
  broken into chunks

Add the first 5 ingredients in a blender. Blend and set aside. Add the rest of the ingredients and toss with the dressing. Serves 6.

NUT-CRUSTED MOZZARELLA
AND SPINACH SALAD

2 C. pecans, toasted
3/4 t. seasoned salt
1 1/2 C. flour
1 egg
1 T. milk
1 lb. mozzarella cheese,
  cut into 8, 1/2-inch
  thick slices
Salt and pepper to taste
1/2 C. + 3 T. olive oil

1 yellow onion, thinly
  sliced
1 red onion, thinly sliced
2 T. minced shallots
1 T. minced garlic
1/4 C. rice wine vinegar
1 T. honey
8 C. spinach, torn into
  bite size pieces

Place the pecans in a blender, and blend until finely chopped. Add 1/2 teaspoon seasoned salt and 1/2 cup flour. Blend until is a coarse meal. Set aside. Whisk the egg and milk together. Set aside. Season both sides of the cheese with salt and pepper. Coat both sides of the cheese with the remaining flour. Then coat each side with the egg and milk mixture. Set aside. In a saucepan, heat 1 tablespoon of the olive oil over medium heat. Add the onions and cook, stirring, until they caramelize, 10 to 12 minutes. Add the shallots and garlic. Cook, stirring for 1 minute. Whisk in the 1/2 cup oil, vinegar and honey. Remove from the heat and salt and pepper. Set aside. In a large frying pan over medium heat, add the 2 tablespoons oil. Pan-fry the cheese until the crust is golden, 1 to 2 minutes per side. Drain on a paper towel. Toss the spinach with the caramelized onion dressing. Place on 4 plates. Add 2 slices of cheese on each plate. Serves 4.

WILTED SPINACH SALAD

1 lb. spinach, torn into bite size pieces
1 lb. bacon, fried, drained and crumbled - 1/2 C. bacon drippings saved
1 onion, sliced thin

8 oz. fresh mushrooms, sliced thin
1/4 C. sugar
3 oz. Italian dressing
3 oz. white vinegar
Seasoned croutons

In a skillet with the bacon drippings, add the onion, and sauté. Add the sugar, dressing and vinegar. In a bowl, add the spinach, bacon and mushrooms. Pour the dressing over. Top with croutons. Serves 6.

"You're a good example of why some animals eat their young."

Jim Samuels

WILTED SPINACH WITH APPLES AND FETA CHEESE

Gary Gardia, St. George, Ut.

8 C. torn spinach
1/4 C. sliced green onions
4 slices bacon
4 T. cider vinegar
1 1/2 t. sugar
1/2 t. dry mustard

1 C. sliced or chopped apple
1/3 C. crumbled feta cheese
2 hard-cooked eggs

In a large bowl, combine the spinach and green onions; set aside. In a large skillet, cook the bacon over medium heat until crisp. Remove the bacon, reserving 2 tablespoons of the drippings in skillet. Drain bacon on paper towels; crumble and set aside. Carefully stir vinegar, sugar and mustard into reserved drippings; bring just to boiling. Add apple and cheese. Toss lightly and transfer to a serving bowl. Remove the yolk from the hard-cooked egg; press yolk through a sieve. Chop the egg white. Sprinkle salad with egg yolk and white and bacon. Serve immediately.

I keep trying to lose weight.....but it keeps finding me!

CONGEALED SPINACH SALAD

1-3 oz. pkg. lemon gelatin
3/4 C. boiling water
1 C. cold water
1 1/2 t. vinegar
1/2 C. mayonnaise
1/2 t. salt

1/3 C. celery, chopped
1 T. onions, minced
1-10 oz. pkg. frozen
   spinach, thawed and water
   squeezed out
3/4 C. cottage cheese

In a large bowl, dissolve the gelatin in the boiling water. Add the cold water. Stir in the vinegar, mayonnaise and salt. Refrigerate until the edges begin to become firm. Beat until fluffy. Add the celery, onion, spinach and cottage cheese to the gelatin mixture. Lightly grease a 1 quart mold. Spoon the spinach mixture into the mold. Cover with plastic wrap and refrigerate overnight. Serves 8.

First you consume chocolate, then chocolate consumes you.

ALL-IN-ONE SALAD BOWL

1-14 oz. can artichoke
  hearts, drained and
  chopped
1 C. green beans, cooked,
  drained and chilled
1/2 Bermuda onion, thinly
  sliced

1 C. peas, cooked, drained
  and chilled
1/2 C. radishes, sliced
2 C. salad greens, broken
1 tomato, cut in 1/8's

DRESSING:
3/4 C. salad oil
1/4 C. vinegar
1/4 t. sugar
Salt and pepper to taste

1 clove garlic, crushed
1 egg, hard-cooked and
  chopped
1/4 C. mustard

Place all the salad ingredients in a bowl. Add the
dressing ingredients in a jar with a lid and mix well.
Pour over the salad and toss. Serves 6.

*You know you are dieting when postage stamps taste
good.*

EAST-WEST SALAD

Leslie Livingston, American Country Collection,
Santa Fe, NM.

1/2 C. slivered almonds
3 T. sugar
1 to 2 heads butter
  lettuce, washed and
  drained

Finely chopped scallions
1 to 2 cans mandarin
  orange slices, in their
  own juice
1 ripe avocado, chopped

DRESSING:
1/4 C. olive oil
1 to 3 drops sesame oil
3 T. rice or cider vinegar
1 to 2 t. cracked black
  pepper

10 to 12 drops Tabasco
  sauce
2 T. sugar
1 T. parsley or dill
Garlic powder to taste

Cook the almonds and sugar over medium heat until sugar caramelizes. Let cool. Mix dressing and keep at room temperature until salad is ready. Mix all the salad ingredients, almonds and dressing and toss.

I'm on a 90-day wonder diet. Thus far, I've lost 45 days.

42

VEGETABLE SALAD

Michelle Cook, Natural Groove, Hitchcock, Tx.

1 carton fresh sliced
  mushrooms
1 head broccoli, chopped
1 head cauliflower,
  chopped
1 small bag radishes,
  sliced

1/2 small purple onion,
  chopped
10 to 12 slices bacon,
  fried and crumbled
1 pkg. ranch dressing mix,
  mixed according to
  package

Mix the dressing mix and place in the refrigerator
until ready to serve. Add all the vegetables and mix
with the dressing.

8-LAYER SALAD

1 head lettuce, chopped
1 C. chopped green onions
1 C. chopped green peppers
1 pkg. frozen peas
1 pt. mayonnaise

3 T. sugar
1/2 lb. bacon, fried and
  crumbled
1 lb. cheddar cheese,
  grated

Layer in a 9x11 inch pan, the ingredients in the order
given. Cover and chill overnight.

*I thought I wanted a career, turns out I just wanted
paychecks.*

MIXED GREENS WITH GOAT CHEESE

1/4 C. red wine vinegar
1 T. Dijon mustard
1 T. chopped fresh thyme
3/4 C. olive oil
Salt and pepper to taste
2-5 oz. bags mixed baby
  greens
1 1/2 C. dried cranberries
1 small red onion, very
  thinly sliced
1 1/2 C. honey-roasted
  pecans
1-5.5 oz. log soft fresh
  goat cheese, crumbled

Whisk the first 3 ingredients in a small bowl. Gradually whisk in the oil. Salt and pepper. Mix the greens, cranberries and onion in a salad bowl. Mix in the dressing and toss. Sprinkle with the nuts and cheese. Serves 10.

WILTED LEAF LETTUCE

Bobbie Williams, Allen, Tx.

2 lg. bunches leaf lettuce
2 T. sugar
2 green onions, sliced
4 slices bacon, fried and
  crumbled
1/4 C. salad vinegar
2 T. water
2 hard-cooked eggs,
  quartered

Tear lettuce into a bowl. Add sugar and the onions. Add the vinegar and water to the bacon drippings. Bring to a boil and pour over the lettuce. Toss until wilted. Add the bacon and eggs. Serves 4.

LETTUCE HEARTS WITH HERBS

4 lettuce hearts
1 T. Dijon mustard
2 T. balsamic vinegar
6 T. olive oil

1 fresh tarragon sprig,
  chopped
4 fresh chives, chopped
Salt and pepper

Cut each lettuce heart into 4. Place all in a salad bowl. Mix the mustard, vinegar, salt and pepper. Gradually whisk in the olive oil. Sprinkle the lettuce with the herbs. Pour the dressing over the salad. Toss and let stand 10 minutes before serving. Serves 4.

BROCCOLI AND CAULIFLOWER SALAD

1 bunch broccoli,
  separated into florets
1 head cauliflower,
  separated into florets
8 slices bacon, fried and
  crumbled

1/3 chopped onion
1 C. tomatoes, chopped
2 hard-boiled eggs, sliced
1 C. mayonnaise
1/3 C. sugar
2 T. vinegar

Add the first 6 ingredients and mix. Mix the sugar, mayonnaise and vinegar until sugar is dissolved. Pour over the salad.

I used up all my sick days, so I'm calling in dead!

ROBIN'S BROCCOLI SALAD

Robin Mantia, Marble Falls, Tx.

6 C. fresh broccoli
 florets, cut into small
 pieces
1 C. roasted sunflower
 seeds

2 T. chopped red onion
1 lb. friend bacon, cut
 into small pieces
1 C. raisins

DRESSING:
1/2 C. mayonnaise
1/2 C. sugar

3 T. apple cider vinegar

Add the salad ingredients and mix. Mix the dressing
ingredients. Pour over the salad and mix.

SWEET BROCCOLI SALAD

1 C. mayonnaise
1/4 C. sugar
2 T. vinegar
8 C. broccoli flowerets
1-11 oz. can mandarin
 oranges

1/2 C. chopped red onion
8 bacon slices, cooked and
 crumbled
1/2 C. raisins
1/2 C. sunflower seeds

In a bowl, whisk the mayonnaise, sugar and vinegar.
Place in the refrigerator and chill for 2 hours. Add
the rest of the ingredients and mix well. Add the
dressing to the salad and mix. Cover and refrigerate
for 1 hour.

SWEET AND CRUNCHY BROCCOLI SALAD

Michael and Peter, Queens Garden,
South Weymouth, Ma.

1 lb. cooked bacon,
  crumbled
1 large head broccoli, cut
  into 1/2-inch pieces
1/2 head cauliflower, cut
  into 1/2-inch pieces

1 medium red onion,
  chopped
1 C. raisins
1-8 oz. bag shredded
  cheddar cheese
1/2 C. sunflower seeds

DRESSING:
1 C. mayonnaise
1/2 C. sugar

2 T. vinegar

Add the salad ingredients and toss. Mix the dressing
ingredients. Pour over the salad and chill. Garnish
with dried parsley.

*If you can smile when things go wrong, you have someone
in mind to blame.*

SPRING SALAD

12 slices bacon, fried and
  crumbled
2 heads fresh broccoli,
  florets only
1 C. celery, chopped
1/2 C. green onions,
  chopped

1 C. seedless green grapes
1 C. seedless red grapes
1/2 C. raisins
1/2 C. blanched slivered
  almonds

DRESSING:
1 C. mayonnaise
1 T. white wine vinegar

1/4 C. sugar

Add all the salad ingredients in a large salad bowl.
Mix the dressing ingredients and pour over the salad.
Toss to coat. Refrigerate until ready to serve. Serves
8.

GREENS WITH GARLIC DRESSING

1 bunch spinach, shredded
6 oz. green beans

4 zucchini, sliced

DRESSING:
6 cloves garlic, unpeeled
1/2 C. olive oil

3 T. red wine vinegar
2 T. chopped parsley

Steam the spinach, beans and zucchini separately, until
they just change color. Drain and place on a serving
platter. Place the garlic in a frying pan over high
heat. Cook until skins are charred. Cool and remove
skins. Place the garlic, oil and vinegar in a blender
and process until smooth. Stir in the parsley and spoon
over the vegetables. Serves 4.

GREEN BEAN SALAD

1 T. olive oil
1-16 oz. pkg. frozen,
 uncooked green beans
4 C. butter head lettuce

1 onion, sliced in rings
2 C. cherry tomatoes,
 sliced in half
2 T. red wine vinegar

Allow the green beans to thaw and drain. Add to the lettuce, onion and tomatoes. Add the olive oil and vinegar to the salad and toss. Serves 4.

MARINATED GREEN BEAN SALAD

2-16 oz. cans green beans,
 drained
1/3 C. vinegar
1/2 C. vegetable oil
1 onion, sliced
1/2 t. salt
1/2 t. pepper

8 slices bacon, fried and
 crumbled
8 hard-boiled eggs, diced
6 T. mayonnaise
4 t. vinegar
4 t. mustard

Combine the first 6 ingredients. Refrigerate overnight. A few hours before serving, add the rest of the ingredients and refrigerate. Serves 8.

The sooner you fall behind, the more time your's have to catch up.

FRESH GREEN BEAN SALAD

1 lb. fresh green beans
Boiling salted water
3 T. vinegar
3 T. vegetable oil

2 onions, thinly sliced
1/2 t. dill seed
1 t. sugar

Cook the beans in the boiling water. Drain, saving 1/4 cup of the water. Mix all the rest of the ingredients to the saved water. Mix with the green beans and refrigerate for several hours. Serves 4.

SWEET AND SOUR BEANS

Carol Adams, Fort Stockton, Tx.

1 C. sugar
1 C. vinegar
1 C. oil

1 T. garlic salt
2 to 3 cans whole green
    beans, drained

Mix all together first 4 ingredients. Pour over green beans. Refrigerate at least 24 hours. Drain and serve. Serves 8 to 10.

When everything is coming your way, you're in the wrong lane.

GREEN BEAN MUSHROOM SALAD

1 can sliced mushrooms,
  drained
1 can French style green
  beans, drained
1 can fancy Chinese
  vegetables, drained
1 1/2 C. celery, sliced on
  slant
1 C. sugar

3/4 C. white vinegar
1 jar chopped pimentos,
  drained
1-#303 can English peas,
  drained
1 can water chestnuts,
  thinly sliced and drained
1 onion, sliced in rings
Salt and pepper to taste

Mix all the ingredients and refrigerate overnight.

CHINESE SALAD

1-#2 can green beans,
  drained
1-#2 can wax beans,
  drained

1-#2 can Chinese mixed
  vegetables, drained
1 can water chestnuts,
  drained
1 C. chopped onion

DRESSING:
1/3 C. oil
2/3 C. wine vinegar
1/2 C. sugar

1 t. seasoned salt
1 t. pepper

Add all the vegetables to a large jar. Mix the dressing
ingredients and add to the vegetables. Place the lid on
the jar and marinate 4 days, turning each day.

SWEET AND SOUR BLACK-EYED PEA SALAD

Joyce Lambert, Fort Stockton, Tx.

3-#2 cans black-eyed peas
1-#2 can sliced or diced
  carrots
1 medium onion, chopped
1 green pepper, chopped
1 red pepper, chopped, or
  1 small can pimentos,
chopped

1 garlic clove, minced
1 small jalapeño pepper,
  seeded and chopped fine
3/4 C. sugar
3/4 C. vinegar
2/3 C. vegetable oil
1 T. Worcestershire sauce
1 can tomato soup

Mix all ingredients and chill. May be heated.

BLACK-EYED PEA SALAD

2 t. onion, minced
2 t. wine vinegar
2 T. salad oil
1 T. cream

1 C. cooked black-eyed
  peas
Salt and pepper to taste
3 strips bacon, cooked and
  crumbled

Mix all the ingredients, except the bacon, and chill.
Before serving, add the bacon.

Growing old is mandatory, but growing up is optional.

BOSTON BEAN SALAD

1 C. canned baked beans
1/4 C. celery, chopped
1 T. bell pepper, chopped
1 t. onion, finely chopped

1/2 t. mustard
1 T. vinaigrette dressing
3 strips bacon, cooked and
  crumbled

Combine all the ingredients, except the bacon; cover and refrigerate until chilled. Add the bacon before serving.

PINTO BEAN SALAD

2 1/2 C. cooked pinto
  beans, drained and rinsed
6 hard-boiled eggs,
  chopped
1 C. cubed longhorn cheese
1/4 C. thin onion rings

2 T. mayonnaise
1 T. chili sauce
1 t. mustard
1/2 C. bacon bits
Salt and pepper to taste

Combine the first 4 ingredients and chill. Mix the rest of the ingredients, except bacon bits. Pour over the bean mixture and toss. Sprinkle the bacon bits. Serves 6.

I don't suffer from insanity, I enjoy every minute of it.

GUANAJUATO-STYLE BEAN SALAD

1-5 oz. can chickpeas,
  drained and rinsed
1-5 oz. can black beans,
  drained and rinsed
1-5 oz. can pinto beans,
  drained and rinsed

1-8 oz. can green beans,
  drained
3 tomatoes, diced
3 red chilies, cut into
  strips
1/2 onion, sliced thin

DRESSING:
2 T. fresh coriander,
  chopped
1/4 C. lime juice

2 T. olive oil
Salt and pepper to taste

Add all the salad ingredients to a salad bowl and mix. Mix the dressing ingredients and whisk. Add to the salad, and let stand for 30 minutes before serving. Serves 6.

The advantage of excercising every day is that you die healthier.

LAYERED SOUTHWEST BEAN SALAD

4 C. shredded iceberg
  lettuce
2-15 oz. cans black beans,
  rinsed and drained
1 C. red onion, chopped

1-4 oz. can diced green
  chili peppers, drained
2 C. red pepper, chopped
2 T. fresh cilantro,
  snipped
3/4 C. tomato, chopped

DRESSING:
1 1/2 C. sour cream
2 T. fresh lime juice
1 t. chili powder

1/2 t. salt
1/4 t. garlic powder

Starting with the lettuce in a 3 quart serving bowl, layer the salad ingredients, except the tomatoes. Mix the dressing ingredients. Cover and refrigerate separately for at least 2 hours, up to 24 hours. When ready to serve, add the tomatoes, drizzle salad dressing over the salad and toss. Serves 12.

PHIL'S PEA SALAD

1 can peas, drained
1 small onion, chopped
1 C. cubed Velveeta cheese

1 tomato, chopped
Mayonnaise

Mix all the ingredients and add enough mayonnaise to mix the ingredients together. Serves 4.

PEA SALAD II

1-16 oz. pkg. frozen peas,
  blanched under hot water
1-6 oz. can Spanish
  peanuts

1/2 pkg. Italian Good
  Seasons dressing mix
2 T. mayonnaise
Sour cream to mix

Combine all the ingredients and chill. Serves 4.

WEEPING SALAD

1 head lettuce
Mayonnaise
1 red onion, sliced
Sugar

1-16 oz. can English peas,
  drained
Swiss cheese, grated
3 slices of bacon, cooked
  and crumbled

In a large salad bowl, tear some lettuce into small
pieces, and place in bowl. Cover with mayonnaise. Add
some of the red onion slices, and sprinkle some sugar
over. Place some of the peas over and top with some of
the Swiss cheese. Add another layer using the rest of
the ingredients. Wrap with foil and refrigerate for 2
hours. Before serving, sprinkle with the bacon.

Hard work has a future payoff. Laziness pays off now!

CONGEALED ASPARAGUS SALAD

2 envelopes unflavored
  gelatin
1/2 C. cold water
1-10 oz. can cream of
  asparagus soup
1/2 C. mayonnaise
3-3 oz. pkg. cream cheese,
  softened

1 T. onion, grated
1 C. stuffed olives,
  sliced
2-10 1/2 oz. cans
  asparagus spears, drained
1/2 C. pecans, toasted and
  broken into pieces

Soften the gelatin in the cold water. Heat undiluted
soup to boiling and add the gelatin mixture. Stir to
dissolve the gelatin. Cool to room temperature. Mix the
mayonnaise and cream cheese. Add to the soup mixture.
Add the rest of the ingredients and mix. Pour into a
mold and chill until set. Serves 10.

ASPARAGUS SALAD MOLD

3/4 C. sugar
1/2 C. vinegar
1 C. water
1 t. salt
1/2 C. cold water
2 envelopes of plain
  gelatin
1 C. celery, chopped
2 T. lemon juice

1 T. onion, minced
1-4 oz. jar pimentos,
  chopped
1 can whole asparagus,
  drained and cut into bite
  size pieces
1-5 oz. can water
  chestnuts, drained and
  sliced thin

In a saucepan, combine the sugar, vinegar, 1 cup of
water and salt. Bring to a boil and dissolve the sugar.
Remove from heat and add the gelatin and onion, and
cool. Combine all the ingredients and put into a mold
and chill.

VINAIGRETTE ASPARAGUS SALAD

1 1/2 lb. fresh asparagus,
  cooked and chilled
3 T. olive oil
4 T. chopped parsley

2 T. chopped chives
2 T. white wine vinegar
1/2 t. salt
Black pepper to taste

Place the asparagus on a serving platter. Mix the rest
of the ingredients and drizzle over the asparagus.
Serves 6.

BLUE CHEESE AND ASPARAGUS SALAD

2 bundles asparagus,
  trimmed and steamed
1/2 C. plain nonfat yogurt
1 T. crumbled blue cheese
1/4 C. fresh lemon juice

1 T. snipped fresh chives
1 garlic clove, minced
2 tomatoes, cut into
  wedges
Salt and pepper to taste

In a small saucepan, add the yogurt and blue cheese.
Warm over low heat for 1 to 2 minutes, whisking
constantly, just until the cheese has melted. Remove
from the heat and whisk in the lemon juice, chives and
garlic. Arrange the asparagus on a platter and ring
with the tomatoes. Drizzle the dressing over the
asparagus. Salt and pepper.

I'm not insensitive, I just don't care.

ASPARAGUS AND HARD-BOILED EGG SALAD

2 shallots, thinly sliced
1 1/2 T. red wine vinegar
1 lb. fresh asparagus,
  trimmed

4 hard-boiled eggs
3 T. olive oil
Salt and pepper to taste

Place the shallots in a small cup and cover them with the red wine vinegar. Set aside. Arrange the asparagus in a large skillet with tips facing the same direction. Add enough cold water to cover. Bring the water to a boil, reduce the temperature and simmer for 5 minutes, just until slightly tender. Drain and rinse under cold water and drain. Arrange in a dish. Drain and rinse the shallots and sprinkle on the asparagus. Cut the eggs in quarters and arrange them around the asparagus. Whisk the olive oil, red vinegar, salt and pepper. Drizzle over the salad. Serves 4.

Every time I think I've hit the bottom, someone lends me a shovel.

ASPARAGUS AND GOAT CHEESE SALAD

1 lb. fresh asparagus
1 head bibb lettuce, torn
3 plum tomatoes, diced
1/2 t. salt

1-3 oz. pkg. goat cheese,
  crumbled
1/4 C. pine nuts, toasted

DRESSING:

2 T. chopped fresh basil
2 T. balsamic vinegar
1 t. sugar

Salt and pepper to taste
1/2 C. olive oil

Snip off tough ends of the asparagus. Cook in salted boiling water 3 minutes. Drain. Plunge in ice water and drain. Arrange the asparagus on the lettuce. Salt the tomatoes. Add on top of asparagus. Add the cheese and nuts. Whisk together all the dressing ingredients, but the olive oil. Slowly add the oil and whisk. Drizzle over the top of the salad. Serves 4.

TINA'S CORN SALAD

Tina Mather-Bothe, Santa Fe Way,
Perrysburg, Oh.

1 can baby white corn,
  drained and cold
3 green onions, chopped
1 tomato, chopped

1 celery stalk, chopped
1/4 C. sour cream
1/4 C. mayonnaise

Add the corn, onions, tomato and celery together. Mix the sour cream and mayonnaise together. Mix the sour cream mixture in the corn mixture and serve.

SHOE-PEG CORN SALAD

5 stalks celery, chopped
1/2 green bell pepper,
  chopped
1 small onion, chopped
2 T. pimento
1 can shoe-peg corn,
  drained

1/2 C. salad oil
2 T. vinegar
1 t. salt
1 t. dry mustard
1 t. sugar

Place the first 5 ingredients in a bowl. In another bowl, add the rest of the ingredients. Mix together with the corn mixture. Place in the refrigerator for at least 1/2 day.

GARBANZO CORN SALAD

12 oz. fresh or frozen
  corn
2 T. olive oil
2 jalapeño peppers,
  grilled, peeled and
  chopped
1 onion, chopped
8 tomatillos, chopped

1/2 C. cider vinegar
1/2 t. black pepper
1 green bell pepper,
  chopped
1-16 oz. can garbanzo
  beans
1 C. chopped cilantro

Sauté the corn in the olive oil for 5 minutes. Add the jalapeño, onions, tomatillos and vinegar to the corn. Simmer for 10 minutes. Remove from the heat and add the black pepper, bell pepper and garbanzo beans. Chill for 1/2 day or more. Add the cilantro before serving.

SQUASH SALAD

2 medium yellow squash,
  thinly sliced
2 medium zucchini, thinly
  sliced

3 C. cooked rice
1/4 red onion, thinly
  sliced

DRESSING:
1/2 C. red wine vinegar
1/2 C. Italian dressing
1 T. chopped parsley

1 T. chopped dill
Salt and pepper to taste

Mix the salad ingredients. Mix the dressing ingredients
and pour over the salad. Chill. Serves 4.

*If at first you don't succeed, give up, no use being a
fool.*

ROASTED VEGETABLE SALAD

1 eggplant, quartered
  lengthwise, sliced into
  1/2-inch pieces
2 small yellow squash,
  halved lengthwise and
  sliced
4 cloves garlic, peeled

1/4 C. olive oil, or as
  needed
1 red pepper, seeded and
  sliced into slices
1 bunch fresh asparagus,
  trimmed and cut into 2-
  inch pieces
1/2 red onion, sliced

DRESSING:
1/4 C. red wine vinegar
2 T. balsamic vinegar
1/4 C. olive oil
2 lemons, juiced

1/4 C. chopped fresh
  parsley
3 T. chopped fresh oregano
Salt and pepper to taste

Preheat the oven to 450 degrees F. Grease a large
baking sheet. Spread the eggplant and squash slices out
on the baking sheet. Place the garlic off to one side
of the pan. Bake for 15 minutes. Whisk together the
first 4 ingredients of the dressing. Add the rest of
the dressing ingredients and mix. Mash the baked garlic
and whisk in the dressing. Set aside. Mix the eggplant
and squash up in the pan and add the asparagus, red
onion and bell pepper on top, and place back in the
oven. Bake for 15 to 20 minutes. When done, place the
vegetables in the dressing. Stir. Chill for a few
hours. Serves 10.

Being good at stupid, doesn't count.

GAZPACHO SALAD

1 envelope unflavored
  gelatin
1/2 C. cold water
1-10 3/4 oz. can condensed
  tomato soup
1 T. vinegar

1/4 t. salt
Dash Tabasco sauce
1 cucumber, peeled and
  chopped
1 green pepper, chopped
1 small onion, chopped

In a saucepan, sprinkle the gelatin over the water. Over low heat, stir until gelatin is dissolved. Remove from the heat. Add the soup, vinegar, salt and Tabasco sauce. Blend well. Chill until slightly thickened. Stir in the rest of the ingredients. Pour into an oiled 3-cup mold. Chill about 2 hours or until set. To serve, unmold. Serves 5.

CUCUMBER AND PEAR SALAD

3 cucumbers, sliced
2 pears, peeled, thinly
  sliced
Fresh lemon juice
7 oz. feta cheese, diced

1 fresh thyme sprig,
  chopped
4 T. olive oil
1 T. balsamic vinegar
Salt and pepper to taste

Blanch the cucumber slices in salted, boiling water for 1 minute. Then put in cold water. Pat dry with a towel. Sprinkle the lemon juice over the pear slices. On a serving plate, add a ring of cucumbers, pears and cheese. Sprinkle with the thyme. Mix the olive oil, vinegar, salt and pepper. Drizzle over the salad. Serves 4.

CUCUMBER SALAD

1 C. sugar
1 C. white vinegar
1/2 C. water
1 T. snipped fresh dill

2 t. salt
4 cucumbers, thinly sliced
1/3 C. sour cream

Add the first 5 ingredients to a saucepan. Bring to a boil over medium heat. Remove from the heat. Place the cucumbers in a large bowl. Pour the vinegar mixture over cucumbers. Cover and refrigerate overnight. When ready to serve, drain and stir in the sour cream. Serves 6.

FETA GREEK SALAD

Romaine lettuce, torn into
  bite size pieces
3 tomatoes, cut up
1 onion, thinly sliced
1 green pepper, seeded and
  chopped

1 cucumber, peeled and
  sliced
1 C. black olives
1/2 lb. feta cheese, cut
  into chunks

DRESSING:
1/4 C. olive oil
2 T. vinegar

1 pinch oregano
Salt and pepper to taste

Mix all the vegetables and chill. Mix the dressing ingredients together and pour over the vegetables. Serves 6.

MARINATED GREEK SALAD

2 C. cauliflower flowerets
2 C. broccoli flowerets
1 C. sliced, fresh
 mushrooms
3/4 C. pitted, ripe olives
3/4 C. salad olives

12 cherry tomatoes
1-8 oz. bottle Italian
 salad dressing
4 oz. feta cheese,
 crumbled

Add all the ingredients to a salad bowl, except the feta cheese. Chill for several hours or overnight. Add the feta cheese just before serving. Serves 16.

MEDITERRANEAN SALAD

1/8 t. black pepper,
 freshly ground
1/8 t. salt
2 T. olive oil
2 T. lemon juice
1/4 C. balsamic vinegar

3 cloves garlic, minced
4 cucumbers, peeled,
 thinly sliced
1/4 C. red onion, thinly
 sliced
4 tomatoes, chopped

Mix the first 6 ingredients and mix well. Mix the next 3 ingredients in a salad bowl. Pour the dressing over the cucumber mixture and toss. Serves 6.

I have teenagers. Pray for me.

MOZZARELLA AND TOMATO SALAD

4 tomatoes, thickly sliced   8 oz. fresh mozzarella
                              cheese, sliced

DRESSING:
1/4 C. olive oil   1 t. sugar
3 T. balsamic vinegar   1 clove garlic, minced
1 T. water   1 T. chopped fresh basil

Arrange tomatoes, alternating with the mozzarella
slices, on salad plates. Mix the dressing ingredients,
except the basil, and shake well. Pour over the
tomatoes and cheese. Garnish with fresh basil.

*My imaginary friend thinks you have some serious
problems.*

TOMATO SALAD

1/2 lb. crusty country-
  style bread
1/3 C. red onion, minced
4 C. chopped ripe tomatoes
1 cucumber, peeled, seeded
  and chopped
1/2 C. torn basil leaves
1/3 C. Italian parsley,
  chopped

1 C. pitted, chopped
  olives
1 C. feta cheese, crumbled
2 t. minced garlic
5 T. olive oil
4 T. wine vinegar
Pepper to taste

Preheat oven to 400 degrees F. Cut the bread into 1
inch slices and place on a pan. Place on a rack in the
center of the oven and bake 20 minutes. Remove from
oven and cool. Mix the rest of the ingredients in a
bowl. Tear the toasted bread into bite size pieces.
Place half of them over the bottom of a 9x13-inch
baking dish. Pour half the salad mixture over. Add the
rest of the bread and then layer the remaining salad.
Cover with plastic wrap and chill for at least an hour.
Serves 8.

If ignorance is bliss, why aren't more people happy?

GAZPACHO-STYLE SALAD

3 tomatoes, cut into 8
  wedges
1 cucumber, thinly sliced

1 green bell pepper,
  coarsely chopped
1 red onion, thinly sliced
3 T. snipped parsley

DRESSING:
1/4 C. salad oil
3 T. vinegar
1 1/2 t. sugar
1 clove garlic, minced
3/4 t. snipped fresh basil

1/4 t. cumin
1/8 t. dry mustard
Dash bottled hot pepper
  sauce

Mix the dressing in a jar with a lid. Shake until well
mixed. Add the salad ingredients to a bowl and pour
dressing over. Toss. Cover and chill. Serves 6.

AVOCADO SALAD

2 avocados, peeled and
  sliced
Juice of 1 lemon
2 tangerines, peeled and
  sliced horizontally
Romaine lettuce
2 tomatoes, sliced

1 scallion, sliced
1 t. parsley sprigs,
  chopped
2 t. Dijon mustard
6 T. olive oil
Salt and pepper to taste

Mix the mustard, olive oil, salt and pepper. Arrange
the lettuce on a platter. Place the tomatoes,
scallions, avocado slices and tangerines on the
lettuce. Sprinkle the parsley over the salad. Drizzle
the salad dressing over the salad. Serves 4.

ARTICHOKE HEARTS SALAD

3 heads Boston lettuce
3 cans artichoke hearts,
 drained and chopped

2 avocados, sliced

Tear lettuce into bite size pieces and place in a salad bowl. Add the other 2 ingredients. Add the dressing. Serves 12 to 14.

DRESSING:
4 T. olive oil
6 T. vegetable oil
2 T. lemon juice

1 t. marjoram
1/2 t. tarragon
1/2 t. salt and pepper

Mix well and pour over the salad. Can be refrigerated until needed.

ARTICHOKE SALAD

1-7 oz. pkg. dry Italian-
 style salad dressing mix
1 C. low fat sour cream
4 C. chopped romaine
 lettuce
1 C. red bell pepper,
 chopped

1 C. broccoli, chopped
1 C. fresh mushrooms,
 sliced
1/4 C. onion, diced
1-14 oz. can artichoke
 hearts, drained and
 chopped

In a small bowl, add the dressing mix and sour cream and mix well. In a large bowl, add the rest of the ingredients. Top with the dressing and toss. Refrigerate until ready to serve. Serves 6.

RICE SALAD

1 C. rice, cooked as
  package directed
1 C. chopped celery
1/3 C. sliced small green
  onions
1/2 C. chopped red bell
  pepper

2 T. Dijon-style mustard
Salt and pepper
2/3 C. plain nonfat yogurt
1/3 C. mayonnaise
2 hard-boiled eggs,
  chopped
2 small tomatoes

Combine first 6 ingredients and mix well. Add yogurt
and mayonnaise and mix. Add eggs and tomatoes. Cover
and chill.

WILD RICE AND FETA SALAD

1-6 oz. pkg. long-grain
  and wild rice
2 oz. feta cheese,
  crumbled
1/2 C. green bell pepper,
  chopped

1/2 C. yellow bell pepper,
  chopped
1/2 C. onion, chopped
1-2 oz. jar diced
  pimentos, drained

DRESSING:
2 T. water
1 T. olive oil

1/4 C. tarragon wine
  vinegar
1/8 t. pepper

Cook the rice according to package directions. Cool
slightly. In a bowl, add the rest of the salad
ingredients. Add all the dressing ingredients together.
Add all the salad, rice and dressing together and
refrigerate. Can be made a day ahead. Serves 6.

EGG SALAD

1/4 C. mayonnaise
2 t. lemon juice
1 t. dried minced onion
1/4 t. salt
1/4 t. pepper

6 hard-boiled eggs,
  chopped
1/2 C. finely chopped
  celery

Mix the first 5 ingredients. Add the next 2 and mix well. Cover and chill.

SIMPLE SLAW

Billie Black, Horseshoe Bay, Tx.

1 bag thin shredded
  cabbage

Honey-roasted peanuts
Poppy seed dressing

Add all and refrigerate.

Everyone is entitled to my opinion.

TEXAS PANHANDLE COLESLAW

Rachel Turner, Ft. Stockton, Tx.

2 pkg. shredded cabbage
8 to 10 green onions
1 large bell pepper
2 pkg. Ramen noodles,
  chicken flavor
1 C. sliced almonds

1/2 C. sunflower seeds
1 C. oil
2/3 C. sugar
1/3 C. vinegar
1 t. salt
1 t. pepper

Mix the oil, sugar, vinegar, salt and pepper and refrigerate. Put noodles and 3 tablespoons butter in a skillet. Brown lightly; add the seeds and almonds and toss. When ready to serve, add all the ingredients and pour over the dressing. Toss and serve.

SOUTHWESTERN SLAW

1/2 head of green cabbage,
  shredded
1/2 head of purple
  cabbage, shredded
1 red bell pepper, cut
  into fine matchsticks

1 yellow bell pepper, cut
  into fine matchsticks
1 green bell pepper, cut
  into fine matchsticks
1 red jalapeño, seeded and
  minced
3 scallions, sliced thin

DRESSING:
3/4 C. mayonnaise
1/2 C. sour cream
1 T. honey

2 T. cider vinegar
1 t. red chili powder

Mix the dressing ingredients together and refrigerate. Mix the rest of the ingredients and pour the dressing over. Toss. Serves 6.

CALYPSO SLAW

1 C. mayonnaise
2 T. sugar
2 T. vinegar
4 T. mustard
1/2 t. celery seed
Salt and pepper to taste
4 C. shredded cabbage

1-12 oz. can Mexicorn,
  drained
1/2 C. chopped onion
1/2 C. cheddar cheese,
  diced
2 T. ripe olives, sliced

The day before serving, mix the first 5 ingredients. Refrigerate. When ready to serve, add the rest of the ingredients in a bowl. Add the dressing and toss. Serves 6.

SPICED APPLE SLAW

Grace Qualls, Lafayette, La.

1-6 oz. ctn. vanilla low
  fat yogurt
1/4 C. apple juice
1 T. cider vinegar
1/4 t. salt

1/4 t. pepper
1 pkg. shredded cabbage
1/4 C. green onion
2 Granny Smith apples,
  chopped

Mix the first 5 ingredients. Mix the rest of the ingredients in a bowl. Mix with the dressing. Chill for at least 4 hours.

TEXAS YELLOW "COLD SLAW"

Gary Gardia, St. George, Ut.

1/4 C. cider vinegar
2 T. dark brown sugar
1/2 t. celery seed
1/2 t. ground turmeric
1/4 t. ground ginger
Pinch of ground allspice
1 small onion, finely
  diced

1/2 small head cabbage,
  coarsely chopped
2 Kirby cucumbers, peeled,
  seeded and diced
1/2 green bell pepper,
  coarsely chopped
3 T. olive oil
Salt and pepper

In a medium saucepan, bring the vinegar, brown sugar, celery seed, turmeric, ginger and allspice to a boil over medium-high heat. Stir in the onion, remove from the heat, and allow to stand for 5 minutes to cool.

Meanwhile, toss the cabbage, cucumber and bell pepper together in a serving bowl. Whisk the olive oil into the cooled vinegar mixture until combined. Pour the onion-turmeric vinaigrette over the vegetables and toss to coat. Season to taste with salt and pepper, and serve.

Life is a test, and I didn't take very good notes.

TROPICAL SLAW

Gary Gardia, St. George, Ut.

2 C. shredded white
  cabbage
1 C. shredded red cabbage
2 C. grated carrot
3 C. chopped celery
1/3 C. chopped dates
1/3 C. dried chopped
  pineapple

2/3 C. lemon or vanilla
  low fat yogurt
3 T. fat free sweet and
  sour vinegar dressing
1/2 C. dry-roasted salted
  peanuts, chopped

In a large bowl, combine the cabbage, carrots, celery, dates and pineapple. Mix in the yogurt and vinegar dressing. Before serving, mix in the salted peanuts. Makes 8 large servings.

If it weren't for stress I'd have no energy at all.

SOUTHWESTERN POTATO SALAD

2 lbs. tiny new potatoes, quartered

1-8 oz. bottle low-calorie ranch salad dressing

2 small fresh jalapeño peppers, seeded and finely chopped

2 T. snipped fresh cilantro or parsley

1 t. lime peel, finely shredded

1/4 t. salt

1/4 t. pepper

1 C. peeled jicama, chopped

1/2 C. sliced ripe olives

1/4 C. green onions, sliced

18 cherry tomatoes, halved

Spinach leaves

1 large avocado

Lime juice

Fresh cilantro sprig

In covered saucepan, cook potatoes in lightly salted boiling water 10 to 15 minutes, or just until tender; drain well and cool. Meanwhile, for dressing, stir together bottled dressing, peppers, snipped cilantro or parsley, lime peel, salt and pepper. In large bowl, combine potatoes, jicama, olives and green onion. Pour dressing over all; toss gently to mix. Cover and chill for 6 to 24 hours, stirring occasionally. Just before serving, toss tomatoes with salad. Transfer to spinach-lined bowl. Halve, seed and peel avocado. Slice avocado and brush with lime juice. Arrange avocado atop potato salad. Garnish with cilantro sprig, if desired. Makes 8 servings.

I can resist everything except temptation.

MEXICAN POTATO SALAD

1 lb. potatoes, cooked
  until just tender
1 large tomato, chopped
1/4 C. green onions,
  sliced

1/4 C. picante sauce
2 T. lime juice
Salt and pepper to taste

Mix the potatoes, tomato and onions together. Place the picante sauce, lime juice, salt and pepper in a bowl and cook in the microwave, uncovered, for 1 minute. Add to the potatoes and mix.

POTATO SALAD WITH ARTICHOKE HEARTS

8 new potatoes
1 can bouillon
1 red onion, chopped
12 cherry tomatoes
1-4 oz. can artichoke
  hearts, drained and
  sliced

1/4 C. parsley, chopped
1/2 t. salt
1/2 t. pepper
1/2 small green pepper,
  chopped
1 C. mayonnaise

Bake the new potatoes and cool. Peel and slice them. Marinate them in the bouillon for 1 hour. Add all the other ingredients, except mayonnaise and potatoes, in a bowl. Just before serving, drain the potatoes and mix with the rest of the ingredients. Add the mayonnaise. Serves 8.

EASY POTATO SALAD

1-24 oz. pkg. frozen
  potato wedges with skins
1 C. celery, sliced
1/2 C. red bell pepper,
  chopped
2 T. green onions, chopped

1/4 t. garlic powder
1/4 t. salt
Black pepper to taste
1/4 C. honey
1/4 C. mustard

Cook potatoes as directed. Drain and cut wedges in half. Add the celery, bell pepper and onions to the potatoes. Mix the rest of the ingredients in a small bowl. Add to the potatoes and mix well. Makes 12 servings.

GERMAN POTATO SALAD

8 slices bacon, cooked and
  crumbled
1/2 C. green onion,
  chopped
1/4 C. white vinegar

2 T. sugar
1 t. salt
6 potatoes, cooked and
  sliced

Add the potatoes and onions together. Add the rest of the ingredients to a small and mix well. Add to the potatoes and serve hot.

If the shoe fits.....buy in every color.

79

SWEET POTATO SALAD

1/2 lb. bacon, cooked and
  crumbled
3 C. cooked sweet
  potatoes, diced
2 C. pineapple chunks
1/2 C. mayonnaise

1 T. mustard
2 T. lime juice
1/2 t. pepper
1/2 C. macadamia nuts,
  chopped

Add the bacon, potatoes and pineapple in a bowl. In a small bowl, add the mayonnaise, mustard, lime juice and pepper. Mix well. Add to the potatoes and mix. Cover and refrigerate. When ready to serve, add the nuts. Serves 6.

CAESAR POTATO SALAD

DRESSING:
1/2 C. salad oil
1/4 C. grated parmesan
  cheese
1/4 C. lemon juice

1 t. salt
1 T. Worcestershire sauce
1/4 t. pepper

SALAD:
5 lbs. potatoes, cooked
8 bacon slices, cooked and
  crumbled

1 small onion, chopped
1/4 C. parsley, chopped
2 hard-boiled eggs, sliced

Add the dressing ingredients together and blend with a fork. Mix all the salad ingredients together, except the eggs, and mix with the dressing. Mix. Add the eggs to the top of the salad. Cover and refrigerate. Serves 10.

BAKED POTATO SALAD

3 T. oleo
3 T. flour
1 t. salt
1 t. mustard
1/2 t. pepper

1 1/2 C. milk
3/4 C. mayonnaise
1 can green beans, drained
6 large potatoes, cooked
  and cubed

Preheat the oven to 350 degrees F. In a saucepan over low heat, melt the oleo. Add the salt, mustard, pepper and milk. Stirring, make a white sauce. Remove from the heat and add the mayonnaise. Add the white sauce to the green beans and potatoes. Add the mixture to a casserole dish and bake for 45 minutes.

RED POTATO SALAD

1 1/2 lbs. new red
  potatoes
1 C. salad dressing
1 T. mustard
1 T. white wine vinegar
2 t. sugar

1/2 t. pepper
1/4 t. salt
1/3 C. sweet relish
1/3 C. green onion, sliced
3 hard-boiled eggs,
  coarsely chopped

Cut the potatoes in quarters. Boil until just tender. Cool. Add the eggs to the potatoes. Add the rest of the ingredients and mix. Add to the potatoes and mix well. Refrigerate for at least 2 hours, up to 24 hours. Serves 10.

MEXICAN POTATO SALAD

1 lb. tiny new potatoes,
  quartered
1/4 C. water
1/4 C. picante sauce
2 T. lime juice
1 T. olive oil
Salt and pepper to taste

1 tomato, chopped
1/2 C. sliced pitted ripe
  olives
1/4 C. green onions,
  sliced
1 T. cilantro, snipped

Place the potatoes and water in a microwave dish. Cover and cook for 7 to 11 minutes until potatoes are tender. Drain. Add the picante sauce, lime juice, oil, salt and pepper in a microwave dish, and cook, uncovered, on HIGH for 1 minute. Add to the potatoes and mix. Stir in the tomato, olives, onions and cilantro. Toss. Serves 4.

WARM GREEN CHILI POTATO SALAD

Gary Gardia, St. George, Ut.

4 large potatoes, cooked,
  diced and kept warm
1-4 oz. can diced green
  chilies
1/3 C. sliced green onions
1/3 C. chopped ripe olives
1/4 C. Dijon mustard

1/4 C. white wine vinegar
1 clove garlic, finely
  chopped
1/3 C. olive oil
1 large hard-cooked egg,
  peeled and chopped

Combine potatoes, chilies, green onions and olives in medium bowl. Combine mustard, vinegar and garlic in small bowl. Slowly whisk in oil. Toss potato mixture and dressing together in large bowl. Season with salt and ground black pepper. Garnish with egg.

Pasta
Salads

SPINACH PASTA SALAD

1-9 oz. pkg. linguine
1-7 oz. pkg. pesto with
  basil
5 C. shredded fresh
  spinach leaves
1 C. chopped fresh tomato

1 C. thinly sliced red
  onion, cut in half
1/4 C. toasted pine nuts
3 T. lemon juice
1/2 t. salt

Cook the pasta according to package. Rinse and drain.
Mix the pesto, spinach, tomato, onion and pine nuts in
a large bowl. In a smaller bowl, add the rest of the
ingredients. Add to the pasta and toss well. Serves 4.

Chocolate. Coffee. Men. Some things are just better rich.

ANGEL HAIR PASTA SALAD

6 oz. angel hair pasta, broken and cooked according to pkg., drained

2 tomatoes, chopped

1 C. broccoli florets

1 C. cauliflower florets

1 C. sliced carrots

2 stalks celery, sliced

1 red pepper, seeded and chopped

1 onion, chopped

1-4 oz. can sliced mushrooms, drained

1-2 1/4 oz. can sliced pitted ripe olives, drained

3 cloves garlic, minced

3/4 C. French salad dressing

1/4 C. snipped fresh parsley

1/4 C. Parmesan cheese, grated

In a large bowl, combine the tomato, broccoli, cauliflower, carrot, celery, sweet pepper, onion, mushrooms, olives and garlic. Add the pasta. Add the salad dressing and toss. Sprinkle with parsley and cheese. Toss again. Chill, covered, for at least 4 hours. Serves 16.

I started out with nothing, and I still have most of it.

PENNE SALAD

1-12 oz. pkg. penne pasta, cooked as directed on pkg.
1/4 C. olive oil
1 bunch green onions, sliced thinly
1 clove garlic, minced
1 C. quartered cherry tomatoes
Salt and pepper to taste
5 oz. Mozzarella cheese, diced
1/2 C. grated Parmesan cheese
4 oz. fresh basil, coarsely torn
12 large black olives, halved

Heat the olive oil in a saucepan. Add the onions and cook, stirring occasionally, 2 to 3 minutes. Stir in the garlic and cook for 2 more minutes. Add the cooked pasta, tomatoes, salt and pepper. Cook over low heat until warm. Stir in the cheeses. Remove from the heat and add the basil and olives. Serve immediately.

MUFFELATTA PASTA SALAD

June Badon, Liberty Hill, Tx.

1-12 oz. pkg. vermicelli spaghetti, boiled 4 minutes
1/2 C. Wesson oil
3 T. Tex Joy seasoning
3 T. lemon juice
Tabasco sauce to taste
2 to 3 T. Worcestershire sauce
1 large jar chopped pimentos, drain some of the juice
1 jar chopped black olives
2 heaping T. mayonnaise

Mix the first 6 ingredients and marinate 3 hours or overnight. When ready to serve, add the rest of the ingredients.

SPAGHETTI SALAD

1-1 lb. box spaghetti,
  cooked, drained and
  cooled
2 tomatoes, chopped

1 onion, chopped
1 green onion, chopped
1 bottle Italian dressing
Salad Supreme to taste

Mix all the ingredients and toss. Chill.

SPAGHETTI AND VEGETABLE SALAD

1 lb. spaghetti
1 C. cucumber, peeled and
  diced
1 C. tomato, diced
1 bunch green onions,
  sliced thin
1 C. celery, diced

1 C. green pepper, diced
12 oz. Swiss cheese,
  grated fine
1/2 bottle Schilling Salad
  Supreme
1-12 oz. bottle Italian
  dressing

Break spaghetti in thirds. Cook as directed. Drain.
Combine all the ingredients and toss. Refrigerate.
Serves 6.

I intend to live forever-so far so good.

BLT MACARONI SALAD

2 C. uncooked macaroni
1 bunch green onions,
  chopped
1 large tomato, chopped
1 1/4 C. celery, diced
1 1/4 C. mayonnaise

5 t. vinegar
1/4 t. salt
1/8 t. pepper
1 lb. bacon, cooked and
  crumbled

Cook the pasta. Drain. Mix all the ingredients, except
the bacon, and toss. Chill for at least 2 hours. When
ready to serve, add the bacon.

CREOLE MACARONI SALAD

8 oz. cooked macaroni,
  rinsed and drained well
2 C. diced tomatoes
3/4 C. shredded Cheddar
  cheese
1 C. mayonnaise

1/4 C. sliced stuffed
  olives
2 T. grated onions
1 clove garlic, finely
  chopped
1/8 t. cayenne pepper

Chill the macaroni. Add the rest of the ingredients and
toss.

Well, aren't you just the most black hole of need!

MEXICAN MACARONI SALAD

SALAD:
1-10 oz. pkg. small elbow
  macaroni, cooked and
  drained
1/2 C. chopped green
  pepper
4 scallions, chopped

1-15 oz. can kidney beans,
  drained
1-12 oz. can corn niblets,
  drained
1/2 C. pimiento-stuffed
  green olives, sliced

DRESSING:
2/3 C. cider vinegar
1/3 C. mayonnaise
1/4 C. oil

2 t. chili powder
1 t. salt

Mix all the salad ingredients together. Mix the dressing ingredients together. Pour over the salad and toss. Cover and refrigerate overnight. Serves 12.

PESTO PASTA SALAD

1-16 oz. pkg. small shell
  pasta
1/2 C. red wine vinegar
1 T. sugar
1 t. seasoned pepper
1/2 t. salt
1 t. Dijon mustard

1 garlic clove, pressed
3/4 C. olive oil
1 C. chopped fresh basil
1-3 oz. pkg. shredded
  Parmesan cheese
1/2 C. toasted pine nuts

Prepare pasta according to package directions. Drain. Whisk the vinegar, sugar, pepper, salt, mustard and garlic. Gradually whisk in olive oil. Add the mixture to the pasta. Add the rest of the ingredients and toss. Serves 8.

SOUTHWESTERN PASTA SALAD

SALAD:

6 oz. bow-tie pasta, cooked and rinsed in cold water, drained

1-16 oz. can black beans, rinsed and drained

1 pt. grape tomatoes, halved

3/4 C. red onion, chopped

1 avocado, peeled and cubed

1 C. frozen corn, thawed and drained

DRESSING:

1/2 C. olive oil

1/3 C. lime juice

1/3 C. fresh cilantro, chopped finely

2 cloves garlic, minced finely

1 T. hot pepper sauce

1 t. cumin

1 t. salt

Mix the salad ingredients well. Whisk the dressing ingredients until well blended. Add the dressing to the salad and toss. Cover and chill for 1 hour. Serves 6.

Life is too short to dance with ugly men.

SOUTHWESTERN PASTA SALAD

Gary Gardia, St. George, Ut.

2 C. corn
2 C. penne, cooked
2 C. tomatoes, chopped
2 C. cucumber, seeded and
 chopped
3/4 C. onions, chopped
3/4 C. cilantro, chopped

2 jalapeño chili peppers,
 seeded and chopped
1-15 oz. can black beans,
 drained
1/2 C. cider vinegar
3 T. olive oil
2 t. granulated sugar
1/2 t. salt

In a large bowl, combine corn, penne, tomatoes, cucumber, onions, cilantro, chilies, beans and vinegar. Let stand at room temperature for 30 minutes to blend flavors, or refrigerate until serving time. Just before serving, in a small bowl, combine oil, sugar and salt; mix well. Add to salad; toss gently.

They say kids brighten the home. That's because they never turn the lights off.

Fruit
Salads

WINTER FRUIT SALAD

1/2 C. sugar
1/2 C. lemon juice
2 t. onion, finely chopped
1 t. Dijon mustard
1/2 t. salt
2/3 C. vegetable oil
1 T. poppy seeds
1 head romaine lettuce,
  torn into bite-size
  pieces

4 oz. Swiss cheese,
  shredded
1 C. cashews
1/4 C. dried cranberries
1 apple, peeled, cored and
  diced
1 pear, peeled, cored and
  diced

Place the first 5 ingredients in a blender and blend well. While the blender is running, add the oil in a slow steady stream until mixture is thick and smooth. Add the poppy seeds and process just a few seconds more. In a large salad bowl, add the rest of the ingredients and pour the dressing over. Toss. Serves 12.

MELON SALAD

2 C. cantaloupe chunks
3 C. honeydew chunks
1 pt. fresh strawberries,
  halved
1-15 1/4 oz. can pineapple
  chunks, drained

1-11 oz. can mandarin
  oranges, drained
1-6 oz. can frozen
  lemonade concentrate,
  thawed and undiluted
1/2 C. orange marmalade

Place the first 5 ingredients in a bowl. Combine lemonade concentrate and marmalade and mix well. Pour mixture over the fruit mixture. Stir gently to coat. Cover and chill at least 2 hours. Serves 8.

CITRUS AND PECAN SALAD

1-10 oz. bag mixed salad
  greens
2-11 oz. cans mandarin
  orange segments, drained
1/2 C. bacon bits

1 C. thinly sliced red
  onions
1/2 C. pecan halves
1/3 C. balsamic
  vinaigrette dressing

Mix all the salad ingredients and toss with the dressing. Serves 6.

IN-SEASON FRUIT SALAD

2 peaches, cut up
1 C. blueberries
1 C. melon balls
3 plums, cut up
1 C. sliced strawberries

1 C. seedless grapes
6 apricots, cut up
2 red apples, cut up
3 bananas, cut up

DRESSING:
1 C. fat-free plain yogurt
3 T. orange juice

1 orange, peeled and seeds
  taken out

Place all the fruit in a bowl. Add the dressing ingredients in a blender and blend until creamy. Pour dressing over the fruit. Serves 8.

AVOCADOS STUFFED WITH FRUIT AND BERRIES

3/4 C. fresh raspberries
2 1/2 t. Dijon mustard
2 T. balsamic vinegar
1 T. honey
1/2 C. olive oil

Salt and pepper to taste
2 1/2 C. mixed berries and
  sliced strawberries
1 C. peeled diced mango
4 ripe avocados

Purée the raspberries with the mustard, vinegar, honey and olive oil in a blender until smooth. Push the dressing through a strainer to remove the seeds. Add the salt and pepper and set aside. Place the fruits in a bowl and gently fold in enough dressing to coat them lightly. Cut the avocados in half, discard the pits and slice a sliver off the bottom of each so they will sit flat. Spoon the fruit in the avocados. Drizzle the salad dressing over each one. Serves 4.

MANGO WALNUT SALAD

3 small mangos, peeled and
  cubed
6 red lettuce leaves, torn
  into pieces
1/2 C. walnut pieces
1/2 C. dried cranberries

1/2 red bell pepper,
  seeded and thinly sliced
1/2 green bell pepper,
  seeded and thinly sliced
1 carrot, peeled and
  sliced

Place all the ingredients in a bowl and toss. Serves 4.

WATERMELON AND MOZZARELLA SALAD

2 C. watermelon balls
2 C. Mozzarella pieces
1 bunch chopped fresh
  basil, leaves only

1 bunch green onions,
  chopped
1/3 c. virgin olive oil
Baby greens

Toss the first 5 ingredients. Serve over a bed of greens. Serves 6.

STRAWBERRY AND PEAR SALAD

8 C. mixed greens
1 pt. fresh strawberries,
  quartered
1/2 C. lightly toasted
  slivered almonds

3 T. chopped red onion
1/4 C. diced orange bell
  pepper
2 firm yellow pears, cored
  and diced

DRESSING:
1/4 C. white balsamic
  vinegar
1/4 C. extra virgin olive
  oil
1/4 t. garlic powder

1/4 t. salt
1 t. lemon-pepper
  seasoning
1 T. lime juice

Toss the salad mixture, except the pears, and refrigerate for 1 hour. Mix the dressing ingredients and shake well. Just before serving, add the pears and pour dressing over the top. Toss to coat. Serves 6.

CRANBERRY SALAD

SALAD:

1-10 oz. pkg. mixed salad
  greens
1 red apple, diced
1 green apple, diced

1 C. shredded Parmesan
  cheese
1/2 C. dried cranberries
1/2 C. slivered almonds,
  toasted

DRESSING:

1 C. cranberries
1/2 C. sugar
1/2 C. cider vinegar
1/4 C. apple juice
  concentrate

1 t. salt
1 t. dried mustard
1 t. grated onion
1 C. vegetable oil

Toss the salad ingredients. In a blender, mix all dressing ingredients, except the oil. Cover and process until smooth. While processing, gradually add oil in a steady stream. Drizzle over salad just before serving. Serves 10.

If life were fair, men would have stretched marks.

GRAPEFRUIT AND BLACK BEAN SALAD

Lettuce leaves
2 grapefruits, peeled and
    thinly sliced and seeded
1-15 oz. can black beans,
    rinsed and drained
1 cucumber, halved
    lengthwise and sliced
1 C. cubed canned papaya,
    drained

2 oz. reduced-fat Monterey
    Jack cheese, cut into 1/
    4-inch cubes
1/2 C. grapefruit juice
3 T. snipped fresh
    cilantro
2 t. honey
1/4 t. ground cumin

Place the lettuce leaves on 4 plates. Arrange the
grapefruit on the plates. Arrange beans, cucumber and
papaya in mounds on lettuce. Sprinkle the cheese on
top. Add all the rest of the ingredients in a screw-top
jar and shake well. Drizzle some of the dressing over
the salad. Serves 4.

FRUIT SALAD ICE

2 small pkg. frozen
    strawberries
1-#2 can crushed
    pineapple, drained

1-#2 1/2 can crushed
    apricots, drained and cut
4 diced bananas
1 C. water
2 C. sugar

Combine the fruits. Cook the sugar and water to make a
syrup, cool and pour syrup over the fruits. Place paper
cupcake liners into a muffin pan. Place the fruit in
the muffin cups and freeze. Remove paper and serve.

FRUIT SALAD WITH AVOCADO DRESSING

SALAD:

1 large mango, peeled and diced

3 apricots, peeled and quartered

3 plums, peeled and quartered

2 C. strawberries, halved

1 small bunch green grapes, stemmed

1 lb. mixed greens

DRESSING:

1/2 avocado, peeled and mashed

1/2 C. plain yogurt

1 T. honey

2 scallions, minced

1/2 t. lemon zest

1/4 t. orange zest

1/4 t. salt

1/4 t. ground cumin

1/8 t. pepper

1/2 t. red jalapeño chili

2 T. light cream

Add all the dressing ingredients in a blender and blend. Add all the salad ingredients in a bowl and toss. Drizzle the dressing over the salad. Serves 8.

FROSTED GRAPE AND RICE SALAD

1 C. sour cream

5 T. brown sugar

1/2 t. cinnamon

2 1/2 C. seeded grapes, cut in halves

2 c. cold cooked rice

Mix the first 3 ingredients. Mix well and refrigerate. When ready to serve, fold the grapes and rice into the dressing mix. Serve on a plate of lettuce leaves. Serves 6.

WALDORF SALAD DELUXE

3 tart apples, cut into
chunks
3 T. lemon juice
1 stalk celery, minced
2 c. seedless grapes,
halved

1 C. Cheddar cheese, diced
1/4 C. minced dates
3/4 C. toasted pecans,
chopped

DRESSING:
1 C. yogurt
1/4 C. mayonnaise

1/2 C. orange juice
1/2 t. grated orange rind

Whisk together the dressing ingredients. Mix all the
salad ingredients and pour the dressing over.

FRUIT SALAD WITH CHAMPAGNE SAUCE

1 C. kiwi, peeled and cut
in 1/4-inch cubes
1 C. figs, peeled and cut
in 1/4-inch cubes
1 C. grapes, halved

1 C. strawberries, halved
1 C. raspberries
2 egg yolks
1/3 C. sugar
1 C. champagne

Mix the sugar and yolks in a mixing bowl. Whisk until
the yolks begin to turn a light lemony color. Add the
champagne, a little at a time, whisking constantly
until well blended. Place the mixing bowl in a pan and
pour about 1-inch of water around it. Bring the water
to a simmer and continue to whisk vigorously until the
mixture becomes light and foamy. Remove from the heat.
Continue to whisk for 10 seconds. Divide the fruit into
4 small ovenproof plates and pour the sauce over. Place
3 inches from the broiler, allow to cook until they are
lightly browned on the surface. Serves 4.

STRAWBERRY POPPY SEED SALAD

1 bunch lettuce leaves
1 pt. basket fresh
 strawberries, stemmed and
 halved

1 small red onion, sliced
 and separated into rings

DRESSING:
1/3 C. vegetable oil
3 T. cider vinegar
2 T. water
1 1/2 T. honey

1 T. poppy seeds
1/2 t. salt
1/2 t. paprika
1/4 t. pepper

Mix all the dressing ingredients in a blender. Blend until thoroughly mixed. Set aside. Arrange all the salad ingredients together and drizzle the dressing over. Serves 4.

PEAR SALAD WITH RASPBERRY CREAM

4 firm, ripe pears,
 quartered
2 T. lemon juice
1 head bibb lettuce, torn
1 small head romaine
 lettuce, torn

1/2 C. shredded Parmesan
 cheese
6 bacon slices, cooked and
 crumbled
1/2 C. fresh raspberries

DRESSING:
3/4 C. sour cream
1/4 C. raspberry preserves

3 T. white wine vinegar
1/8 t. Dijon mustard

Whisk together the ingredients in the dressing. Set aside. Brush the pears with the lemon juice. Arrange the lettuce on 4 plates. Arrange pears over lettuce. Drizzle with the dressing. Sprinkle with cheese, bacon and raspberries. Serves 4.

RED ONION AND ORANGE SALAD

DRESSING:
1/2 C. honey
1/4 C. rice vinegar

1 T. caraway seeds

SALAD:
6 large navel oranges,
  peeled and thinly sliced

1 large purple onion,
  thinly sliced and
  separated into rings
Fresh cilantro

Whisk together the dressing ingredients. Arrange the orange slices and onion slices on a large serving platter. Insert the cilantro sprigs among the slices. Drizzle the dressing over the salad. Cover and refrigerate for 3 hours. Serves 6.

CRANBERRY SALAD

4 C. fresh cranberries,
  ground in food processor
2 C. sugar
1-20 oz. can crushed
  pineapple, undrained

1/2 C. pecans, chopped
1 C. heavy cream, whipped
1 C. miniature
  marshmallows

Mix the cranberries and sugar and let stand for 2 hours. Add the pineapple and pecans. Mix well. Fold in the whipped cream and marshmallows. Refrigerate overnight. Serves 12.

SUMMER SALAD

DRESSING:

1-8 oz. ctn. nonfat plain
  yogurt
2 T. thawed orange juice
  concentrate

2 T. fresh basil, chopped
1 T. honey

SALAD:

1 head iceberg lettuce,
  cut into 8 wedges
8 fresh apricots, halved
  and pitted
1 pt. basket fresh
  strawberries, sliced in
  half

1 cantaloupe, peeled,
  seeded and sliced
1/4 C. shelled and chopped
  pistachios

Whisk all the ingredients of the dressing. Place 2
wedges of the lettuce on each plate. Place all the
fruit and nuts on top. Drizzle the dressing over.
Serves 4.

Seven days without chocolate makes one weak.

MARGARITA FRUIT SALAD

DRESSING:
3 T. tequila
3 T. triple sec

3 T. orange marmalade
Juice of 1 lime, 2 T.

SALAD:
4 C. fresh strawberries,
  sliced
4 oranges, peeled,
  sectioned and cut in
  small pieces

1 small honeydew melon,
  rind and seeds removed
  and cut into small pieces

Mix the dressing in a bowl. Add the fruit and stir
well. Refrigerate overnight. Serves 6.

7-UP SALAD

1 pkg. cream cheese,
  softened
1 C. boiling water
1 small pkg. lemon Jell-o
1 t. vanilla

1 small can crushed
  pineapple, drained
1 t. sugar
1 C. 7-Up, cold
1 C. pecans, chopped

Mix the cream cheese, Jell-o and boiling water. Mix
well. Add the rest of the ingredients. Serves 4.

AUTUMN FRUIT SALAD

2 red Delicious apples,
  cored and cut into chunks
1 sliced banana
1 Granny Smith apple,
  cored and cut into chunks
2 Bartlett pears, cored
  and cut into chunks
1/2 lb. red seedless
  grapes, cut into halves

1/2 C. toasted almond
  slivers
1 C. vanilla yogurt
1 t. cinnamon
1/4 t. ginger
1/2 t. nutmeg
1 T. apple cider

Combine the fruits and almonds in a salad bowl. Mix the rest of the ingredients. Pour over the fruit. Chill. Serves 8.

SPARKLING FRUIT BOWL

2 oranges, peeled and
  sliced
2 C. mangos, peeled and
  sliced

2 C. melons, peeled and
  cut into chunks
2 C. whole berries, your
  choice

DRESSING:
1 C. chilled carbonated
  water
1/4 C. honey

1 T. lemon juice
1 t. orange zest

In a large serving bowl, arrange oranges on bottom. Add the rest of the fruit on top. Add all the dressing ingredients together and mix. Pour over the fruit. Serves 8.

ORANGE AND WALNUT GREEN SALAD

Grace Qualls, Lafayette, La.

DRESSING:

1/2 C. orange juice

1 T. olive oil

1/4 t. salt

Dash of hot sauce

SALAD:

6 to 8 C. assorted lettuce
  leaves

2 navel oranges, peeled
  and sectioned

1/2 red onion, thinly
  sliced

1/4 C. chopped walnuts,
  toasted

Mix the dressing ingredients well. Mix the salad ingredients in a bowl. Pour the dressing over the salad. Serves 8.

STRAWBERRY AND KIWI SALAD WITH POPPY-SESAME DRESSING

8 C. mixed greens

1 pt. strawberries, sliced

3 kiwis, peeled and sliced

DRESSING:

1/3 C. sugar

1 T. poppy seeds

1 T. sesame seeds

1 T. onion, minced

1/3 C. raspberry vinegar

1/4 C. balsamic vinegar

2 T. olive oil

Mix the dressing and refrigerate. When ready to serve, toss the greens, strawberries and kiwis. Pour dressing over and toss. Makes 8 servings.

ANGEL HASH SALAD

2 T. cornstarch
1/4 C. sugar
1-20 oz. can pineapple
  tidbits, drained and save
  syrup
1 C. pineapple syrup +
  enough water for 1 C.

2 egg yolks
1 C. heavy cream, whipped
1/4 C. chopped walnuts
15 marshmallows, quartered
6 bananas, sliced
Leaf lettuce

Combine cornstarch, sugar, syrup and egg yolks in saucepan. Mix well. Cook over medium heat until thickened. Cool. Fold the whipped cream into the egg mixture. Add the pineapple tidbits, walnuts, marshmallows and bananas. Chill. Serve on the lettuce.

FRESH CRANBERRY SALAD

Marsha Knapp, Natural Groove, Hitchcok, Tx.

1 lb. fresh raw
  cranberries
1 medium orange
1 medium apple, peeled,
  cored and chopped fine

1 C. pecans, chopped fine
2 pkg. large raspberry
  Jell-o
2 C. sugar

Prepare Jell-o as directed on box. Put the cranberries and orange, peel and all, through a food processor or blender. Mix with the sugar. When the Jell-o cools, add all the ingredients and stir. Pour into desired mold or pan. Refrigerate overnight. Serves 8 to 10.

LIME-LEMON SALAD

Michelle Cook, Natural Groove, Hitchcok, Tx.

1-3 oz. pkg. lime Jell-o
1-3 oz. pkg. lemon Jell-o
2 C. hot water
1 large can crushed
  pineapple
1 large carton cottage
  cheese

1 C. mayonnaise
1/2 can sweetened
  condensed milk
1 C. pecans, coarsely
  chopped

Dissolve Jell-os in hot water. Add the remaining ingredients in order. Pour into an 8 x 12 1/2-inch pan. Cover and refrigerate until firm. Slice and serve on lettuce. Makes 20 square cuts.

SNICKER SALAD

Jeanne Meaike, Audubon, Ia.

3 red or green apples,
  diced
1 small pkg. sugar free
  vanilla pudding
1 C. milk

1 C. small marshmallows
6 large Snicker candy
  bars, cut into small
  pieces
1 ctn. whipped cream

Mix the pudding, milk and whipped cream. Add the apples and Snickers into the pudding mixture. Stir in the marshmallows. Yummy and easy!

CHERRY PIE SALAD

Diana Ballou, Audubon, Ia.

1 can cherry pie filling
1 large pkg. cherry
 gelatin

2 C. boiling water
1 C. cold water

Dissolve the gelatin in the hot water. Stir in the cold water. Slowly stir in the cherry pie filling. Refrigerate until set. May use as a salad or add Cool Whip for a dessert.

BLUEBERRY SALAD

Diana Ballou, Audubon, Ia.

1 can blueberry pie
 filling
1 small can crushed
 pineapple, drained

2-3 oz. pkg. grape gelatin
2 C. boiling water
1 C. cold water

Dissolve the gelatin in the hot water. Stir in the cold water. Stir in the pineapple and blueberry pie filling. Refrigerate until set. May be used as a salad or add Cool Whip for a dessert.

Don't believe everything you think.

STAINED GLASS FRUIT SALAD

Joyce Lambert, Fort Stockton, Tx.

1-20 oz. can peach pie
  filling
2-11 oz. cans mandarin
  oranges, drained

1-20 oz. can chunk
  pineapple, drained
3 medium bananas, sliced

Mix and chill.

PRETZEL SALAD

Joyce Lambert, Fort Stockton, Tx.

2 C. crushed pretzels
1/4 C. sugar
1 1/2 sticks margarine,
  melted
8 oz. cream cheese
1 C. sugar
1 1/2 C. Cool Whip

1-6 oz. pkg. strawberry
  gelatin
1 large can crushed
  pineapple, drained, save
  juice
2-10 oz. boxes frozen
  strawberries, drained,
  save juice

Mix pretzels, 1/4 cup sugar and margarine. Press in a
9x12-inch dish. Bake 10 minutes at 350 degrees F. Mix
the cream cheese, 1 cup sugar and fold in the Cool
Whip. Spread over the cooled pretzel crust. Dissolve
gelatin in hot pineapple and strawberry juice, adding
enough water to make 2 cups. Put in the refrigerator
until gelatin is syrup and then add the fruits. Spread
over the top of cream cheese. Chill well.

STRAWBERRY PRETZEL SALAD

Gary Gardia, St. George, Ut.

2 C. crushed pretzels
3/4 C. melted butter
3 T. sugar + 3/4 C. sugar
1-8 oz. pkg. cream cheese
1-8 oz. ctn. whipped
  topping
2-3 oz. pkg. strawberry
  gelatin dessert mix

2 c. boiling water
2-10 oz. pkg. frozen
  strawberries
1-8 oz. can crushed
  pineapple
Whipped topping or whipped
  cream to garnish

Preheat oven to 400 degrees F. For the crust, mix the pretzels, butter and 3 tablespoons of sugar. Press this mixture into a 9x13-inch pan and bake for 7 minutes. Set aside and allow to cool. In a mixing bowl, beat together the cream cheese and 3/4 cup of sugar. Fold in the whipped topping and spread over the cooled crust. Refrigerate until well chilled. In a small bowl, dissolve the gelatin in the boiling water and allow to cool slightly. Add the strawberries and pineapple, and pour over the cream cheese mixture. Refrigerate until serving time. To serve, cut slices and serve with a dollop of whipped topping.

If a man's home is his castle, he can learn to clean it!

APRICOT CONGEALED SALAD

Rhonda Roederer, Metarie, La.

1 or 2 cans apricots, drained and juice saved
1 small can crushed pineapple, drained and juice saved

3/4 C. small marshmallows
2 pkg. orange Jell-o
2 C. boiling water

TOPPING:
1/2 C. sugar
3 T. flour
1 egg

1 C. fruit juice
2 T. butter
1/2 pt. whipped cream

Cut the apricots into small pieces. Dissolve the Jell-o with the boiling water. Add the marshmallows and 1 cup of the fruit juice. Stir and refrigerate. When jelling begins, add the apricots and pineapple. Place in the refrigerator. Mix the flour and sugar. Beat the egg with the juice, add water if needed to make 1 cup. Add the butter and cook until thick in a double boiler. Let cool. Beat cream and fold into mixture when cooled. Spread on the Jell-o. Serves 8 to 10.

APRICOT CONGEALED SALAD II

1-8 oz. can crushed pineapple
1-3 oz. box apricot gelatin

1 C. buttermilk
1-8 oz. ctn. Cool Whip
1/2 C. walnuts, chopped

Heat the crushed pineapple and gelatin until dissolved. Refrigerate until cooled. Add the buttermilk, Cool Whip and nuts. Refrigerate until set. Serves 10.

DAIQUIRI FRUIT SALAD

1 1/2 C. crushed
  pineapple, drained,
  saving syrup
1-3 oz. pkg. lime gelatin

1/2 C. frozen limeade
  concentrate, thawed
1/3 C. mayonnaise
2 C. whipped cream
2 medium bananas, sliced

Add enough water to the syrup to make 1 cup. Add to the saucepan and bring to a boil. Add the gelatin and stir in the lime gelatin until dissolved. Add the limeade and salad dressing, stirring until well blended. Chill until slightly thickened but not set, about 45 minutes. Fold in pineapple and remaining ingredients. Pour into an oiled 1 1/2 quart ring mold. Freeze until firm, about 2 hours. To serve, unmold.

I got my exercise running to the refrigerator.

CRANBERRY SALAD MOLD

2-6 oz. pkg. strawberry-
  flavor gelatin
5 oranges, peeled and
  chopped

1-16 oz. pkg. cranberries,
  coarsely chopped
2 C. sugar

DRESSING:
1-8 oz. pkg. cream cheese
1/3 C. orange juice

2 t. grated orange peel
Dash of salt

Dissolve gelatin in 3 cups boiling water. Stir in 3
cups cold water. Refrigerate, stirring often, until
mixture mounds slightly when dropped from a spoon.
Place the oranges, cranberries and sugar in another
bowl. Mix until sugar is dissolve. Stir fruit mixture
into the gelatin. Pour in a bundt cake pan. Refrigerate
until set. Unmold onto a platter with lettuce leaves.
With a mixer on low speed, beat the cream cheese and
orange juice until smooth. Stir in the orange peel and
salt. Pour over the mold. Makes 16 servings.

TOMATO-RASPBERRY ASPIC

Joyce Lambert, Fort Stockton, Tx.

3-3 oz. pkg. raspberry
  Jell-o
1 1/2 C. hot water

3-1 lb. cans stewed
  tomatoes
6 drops Tabasco sauce

Dissolve Jell-o in hot water. Blend tomatoes in food
processor and stir into Jell-o. Add the Tabasco sauce.
Pour into shallow pans, 2 or 3 (9x12-inch). Chill well,
slice and serve.

HOT CURRIED FRUIT

Bobbie Williams, Allen, Tx.

1-29 oz. can apricot
  halves, drained
1-29 oz. can pear halves,
  drained
1-29 oz. can peach halves,
  drained

1-20 oz. can pineapple
  chunks, drained
3/4 C. golden raisins
1/4 C. margarine
1/2 C. packed brown sugar
1 t. curry powder

In a 2 1/2 quart casserole, combine the fruit and
raisins. Melt the butter in a small pan. Stir in the
brown sugar and curry powder. Cook and stir over low
heat until sugar is dissolved. Pour over fruit mixture
and mix gently. Cover and bake at 400 degrees F. for 30
minutes. Serves 12.

ORANGE CREAM FRUIT SALAD

Bobbie Williams, Allen, Tx

1-20 oz. can pineapple
  tidbits, drained
1-16 oz. can peach slices,
  drained
1-11 oz. can mandarin
  oranges, drained
2 medium firm bananas,
  sliced

1 medium apple, chopped
1-3.4 oz. pkg. instant
  vanilla pudding mix
1 1/2 C. milk
1/3 C. frozen orange juice
  concentrate
3/4 C. sour cream

In a large salad bowl, combine fruits. Set aside. In
another small bowl, beat pudding mix, milk and orange
juice concentrate for 2 minutes. Add the sour cream and
mix well. Spoon over fruit. Toss to coat. Cover and
refrigerate for 2 hours. Serves 8.

Notes

Meat
and
Seafood
Salads

PAN-FRIED CHICKEN AND SPINACH SALAD

Suzy Garvey, Treasure Seakers, Charlotte, Nc.

4 skinned and boned
  chicken breast
1/4 C. flour
1 large egg, beaten
2/3 C. Italian-seasoned
  bread crumbs
1/4 C. olive oil
1-6 oz. pkg. fresh baby
  spinach, thoroughly
  washed

1 large apple, thinly
  sliced
1/2 C. walnut pieces
1-8 oz. jar poppy seed
  dressing
1/2 C. sweetened dried
  cranberries
1/2 C. crumbled blue
  cheese

Dredge the chicken in the flour. Dip in the egg and dredge in bread crumbs. Cook in hot oil in a large skillet over medium heat 3 to 5 minutes on each side. Remove from skillet and let stand 5 minutes. Cut chicken diagonally in 1/2-inch-thick slices. Toss together baby spinach, apple slices and nuts. Divide between 4 serving plates, topping evenly with the cooked chicken. Stir together poppy seed dressing, cranberries and blue cheese. Serve the dressing with the salad.

It's not the minutes spent at the table that put on weight, it's the seconds.

CHICKEN SALAD

Grace Qualls, Lafayette, La.

3 C. cooked chicken
  breast, finely cut up
1 C. sectioned purple
  grapes
1/2 C. roasted pecans,
  chopped

3/4 C. finely diced celery
1/2 C. diced pineapple
Curry powder
mayonnaise

Mix all. Add enough mayonnaise to hold together.

CURRIED CHICKEN SALAD

4 cooked skinless,
  boneless chicken breasts,
  diced
3/4 C. chopped celery
1/2 C. chopped onion
1/4 C. nonfat mayonnaise
1/4 C. plain nonfat yogurt

1 t. lemon juice
1 T. soy sauce
1/4 t. curry powder
1/4 C. chopped almonds,
  toasted
1/2 C. thawed frozen green
  peas

Mix the chicken, celery and onion in a bowl. Blend the
mayonnaise, yogurt, lemon juice, soy sauce and curry
powder. Mix with the chicken. Before serving, fold in
the almonds and peas. Serves 4.

HOT CHICKEN SALAD

Michelle Cook, Natural Groove, Hitchcock, Tx.

1 whole chicken, boiled, de-boned and cubed
1 C. Hellmann's mayonnaise
1/2 green bell pepper, chopped
1/2 onion, chopped

2 C. shredded cheese, 1 C. inside, 1 C. on top
1 can water chestnuts, drained
1 jar small mushrooms, drained
1 can French fried onions

Mix together all, except the French fried onions and 1 cup cheese. Place in a baking dish and cover with 1 cup cheese. Bake 25 minutes. Then add the fried onions to cover the top and bake for 5 minutes.

A diet is when you have to go to some length to change your width.

SOUTHWESTERN CHICKEN SALAD

6 chicken breasts, boiled
  and cut into bite-size
  pieces
1/4 C. canned corn
1/2 can black beans,
  drained and rinsed
1-4 oz. can diced green
  chilies

2 celery stalks, diced
1 bunch green onions,
  diced
1-4 oz. jar pimentos,
  drained
1/2 bunch cilantro,
  chopped

DRESSING:
1 1/2 C. mayonnaise
1/4 C. Dijon mustard
2 T. black pepper
1 t. salt
1 T. chili powder

1 T. dill weed
1 T. garlic powder
1 T. sugar
1 T. minced onions

Mix the dressing. Place all the salad ingredients
together and drizzle over the salad. Toss. Chill.

Always remember you're unique, just like everyone else.

CHOP SUEY SALAD

1-13 1/2 oz. can chicken
  broth
1 C. rice
1 1/2 t. salt
1/2 C. vegetable oil
2 T. soy sauce
2 T. toasted sesame seeds
2 C. diced cooked chicken

1-14 oz. can chop suey
  vegetables, drained
1-4 1/2 oz. jar sliced
  mushrooms, drained
4 green onions, sliced
1-2 oz. jar diced pimento,
  drained

Add enough water to broth to make 2 1/2 cups liquid.
Bring to a boil. Stir in rice and 1 teaspoon salt.
Cover and simmer 20 minutes. Remove from heat. Let
stand, covered, until all liquid is absorbed, about 5
minutes. Place rice in a large bowl. Mix the rest of
the salt, oil, soy sauce and sesame seeds, and mix with
rice. Cover and refrigerate for at least an hour. Stir
in the remaining ingredients and stir. Cover and chill
for 3 to 4 hours. Serves 6.

*I know that there are people who do not love their
fellow man, and I hate people like that!*

CHICKEN SALAD MOLD

2 1/2 C. diced cold
  chicken
1 C. finely chopped celery
1 C. sliced white grapes
1 1/2 C. shredded browned
  almonds
2 T. minced parsley

1 t. salt
1 C. mayonnaise
1/2 C. whipping cream,
  whipped
1 1/2 T. gelatin
4 T. water
1/2 C. chicken stock, hot

Soak gelatin in cold water for 5 minutes and dissolve
in the hot chicken stock. Allow to cool. Add the rest
of the ingredients and mix well. Mix with the gelatin
mixture and stir. Press into a mold. Allow 3 to 4 hours
in the refrigerator.

If we weren't all crazy, we would go insane.

PEAR AND CHICKEN SALAD

12 oz. fresh asparagus
  spears, cooked crisp-
  tender
2 pears, halved lengthwise
  and cored

Lemon juice
4 skinless, boneless
  chicken breast halves
Salt and pepper to taste
6 C. torn salad greens

DRESSING:
1/2 C. plain fat-free
  yogurt
1/4 C. red onion, chopped

2 T. crumbled blue cheese
1 T. snipped fresh chives
1/8 t. ground white pepper

Mix the dressing ingredients together. Cover and chill.
Brush the cut sides of the pears with lemon juice. Set
aside. Season the chicken with the salt and pepper. On
a medium-high grill, place the chicken and grill for 5
minutes. Turn chicken. Add the pears, cut sides down.
Grill chicken and pears for 7 to 10 minutes. Add
asparagus the last 3 minutes. Slice the chicken. Cut
the pears in 8 quarters. Add the salad greens on 4
dinner plates and place the chicken and asparagus on
top. Spoon over the salad. Add the pears. Serves 4.

Nobody notices what I do, until I don't do it.

TOASTED PECAN AND CHICKEN SALAD

4 C. diced cooked chicken
2 C. diced celery
1-4 1/2 oz. jar whole
  mushrooms, drained

1/2 C. toasted pecan
  halves
4 slices fried bacon,
  crumbled

DRESSING:
1 C. mayonnaise
1 C. sour cream

1 1/2 t. salt
2 T. lemon juice

Toast pecans in a shallow baking pan in a preheated 350
degree F oven for 15 minutes. Mix all the dressing
ingredients. Mix all the salad ingredients together.
Toss with the dressing. Chill for at least 1 hour.
Serves 6.

I pretend to work. They pretend to pay me.

SANTA FE CHICKEN SALAD

DRESSING:
1/2 C. mayonnaise
1 T. lime juice

2 t. finely-chopped canned
   chipotle chilies in adobo
   sauce

SALAD:
2 1/2 C. chopped cooked
   chicken
1/4 C. finely chopped
   celery
1/4 C. snipped fresh
   cilantro

3 T. thinly-sliced green
   onions
3 T. finely chopped yellow
   sweet pepper
3 T. finely chopped red
   sweet pepper
Salt and pepper to taste

Mix the dressing and set aside. Mix all the salad
ingredients and pour the dressing over. Toss. Cover and
refrigerate for 1 to 4 hours.

Sorry...yesterday was the deadline for all complaints.

COBB SALAD

DRESSING:

1/2 C. olive oil	1/2 t. sugar
1/3 C. red wine vinegar	1/2 t. dry mustard
1 T. lemon juice	1/2 t. pepper
1 t. Worcestershire sauce	1 clove garlic, minced
1/2 t. salt	

SALAD:

6 C. shredded lettuce	6 slices bacon, crumbled
3 C. chopped cooked chicken	3 hard-cooked eggs, chopped
1 1/2 C. tomatoes, chopped	1 avocado, peeled, seeded and cut into wedges
3/4 C. blue cheese, crumbled	

Add the salad ingredients together, placing the avocado wedges on top. Mix all the dressing ingredients in a jar with a lid. Shake well and drizzle over the salad. Serves 6.

A great education has made me what I am today – Stressed!

CAESAR CHICKEN SALAD

2 cloves garlic, minced
  and divided

2 T. olive oil
2 C. cubed French bread

DRESSING:

1/4 C. salad oil
1/4 C. frozen egg product,
  thawed
2 T. red wine vinegar

1 T. lemon juice
1 t. anchovy paste
1/2 t. Worcestershire
  sauce

SALAD:

6 C. torn romaine
2 C. cubed cooked chicken
4 green onions, bias
  sliced

1/4 C. finely shredded
  parmesan cheese
Coarsely ground pepper to
  taste

In a skillet over medium heat, cook 1 clove garlic in
the olive oil. Add the bread, stirring to coat evenly.
Place on a shallow baking pan and bake in a preheated
300 degree F oven for 10 minutes. Stir. Bake about 5
more minutes.

Mix the dressing ingredients in the blender plus 1
clove garlic and blend until smooth. Add the salad in a
large salad bowl, pour dressing on top and toss. Add
the croutons. Add the pepper. Serves 6.

*If it weren't for the last minute, nothing would ever
get done.*

CALIFORNIA CHICKEN SALAD

1 cubed cooked chicken
  breast
2 apples, cored and
  chopped
3 stalks celery
1/2 C. green onions,
  chopped

2 T. parsley, chopped
1/4 C. chopped walnuts,
  toasted
6 C. torn mixed salad
  greens

DRESSING:
1/4 C. sour cream
1/4 C. red wine vinegar
3 T. mayonnaise

1/2 t. sea salt
Ground pepper to taste

Mix the dressing together. Add all the salad
ingredients, except the salad greens, and mix with the
dressing. Divide the salad greens on 6 plates and place
the chicken mixture on top. Serves 6.

*The sooner you fall behind, the more time you'll have
to catch up.*

CHICKEN CHOPPED SALAD

2 heads iceberg lettuce, thinly sliced
3/4 C. pitted Kalamata olives, chopped
1 grilled chicken breast half, chopped

1/2 C. chopped pepperoni
3 roma tomatoes, chopped
1/2 C. shredded fresh basil
1 C. grated Mozzarella cheese

DIJON VINAIGRETTE:
1 egg yolk
3 T. Dijon mustard
1/2 T. honey
1/2 C. red wine vinegar

1 1/2 T. Worcestershire sauce
Salt and pepper to taste
1 1/2 C. olive oil

Mix all the dressing ingredients, except olive oil, in a blender. While the blender is running, gradually pour in the olive oil.

Mix the salad ingredients together. Pour 1 cup of the dressing over the salad and toss. Serves 4.

Someday is not a day of the week.

FRUIT AND CHICKEN SALAD

1 1/2 lbs. boneless,
  skinless chicken breast,
  cooked and cubed
3 C. torn romaine lettuce
3 C. torn spinach leaves
1 C. fat-free chicken
  broth
2 oranges, peeled and cut

1 pink grapefruit, peeled
  and cut
2 ribs celery, finely
  sliced
1/2 ripe avocado, peeled
  and cubed
1/8 C. toasted slivered
  almonds

DRESSING:
1/3 C. orange juice
2 T. olive oil
1 T. white vinegar

1 T. honey
1 t. celery seed

Mix all the dressing ingredients in a jar with a lid.
Shake well. Mix all the salad ingredients in a bowl and
pour dressing over. Toss. Refrigerate 1 to 2 hours.
Serves 6.

I took an IQ test and the results were negative.

ROGER'S FAVORITE CHICKEN SALAD

Allison Saba, Chandler, Az.

1 roasted chicken, boned
  and cubed
1 C. pecan halves
8 scallions, chopped
2 stalks celery, diced

8 oz. Fiji apple, peeled
  and diced
5 T. raisins
1 T. fresh oregano leaves,
  chopped
Salt and pepper to taste

DRESSING:
1/2 C. mayonnaise
2 T. sour cream

1/4 C. cider vinegar

Mix the first 8 ingredients in a serving bowl. Mix the
dressing ingredients well and toss into salad, coating
evenly.

TURKEY SALAD POLYNESIAN

3 C. cooked and cubed
  turkey
1-15 1/4 oz. can pineapple
  chunks, drained
2 ribs celery, thinly
  sliced
3/4 C. mayonnaise

2 T. chopped chutney
1 t. curry powder
1 banana
1/2 C. salted cashews
1/2 C. flaked coconut
1-11 oz. can mandarin
  oranges, drained

Add the first 6 ingredients and mix. Cover and chill.
When ready to serve, add the bananas and cashews and
mix well. Serve in a pineapple shell and sprinkle with
the coconut and oranges. Serves 4.

TURKEY FRUIT SALAD

DRESSING:
1/3 C. plain nonfat yogurt
1 T. light mayonnaise
1 T. honey
1/2 t. orange peel, finely shredded

SALAD:
1 C. cooked turkey, cubed
1 C. fresh strawberries, halved
1 banana, sliced
1/2 C. celery, sliced
2 oranges, peeled and cut
4 lettuce leaves

Combine the dressing and mix. Combine the remaining ingredients, except the lettuce leaves, in a bowl. Fold in the dressing with the salad ingredients. Chill. Spoon on the lettuce leaves. Serves 4.

SANTA FE SMOKIN' RICE SALAD

Gary Gardia, St. George, Ut.

3 C. rice, cooked, cooled to room temperature
1 1/2 C. smoked Gouda cheese, shredded
1 C. smoked turkey breast cubes
2 medium plum tomatoes, coarsely chopped
1/4 medium red onion, cut into 1/2-inch slices
1/2 C. creamy garlic-cilantro salad dressing (or ranch dressing mixed with
1 T. chopped fresh cilantro)
Salt to taste
Pepper to taste

Combine rice, cheese, turkey, tomatoes and onion in a large bowl. Add salad dressing and toss lightly. Season to taste with salt and pepper.

SEVEN-LAYER CHILI SALAD

1-15 oz. can chili with
  beans, heated
4 C. lettuce, torn into
  bit-size pieces
1 C. tomatoes, diced

1 C. onions, diced
2 1/2 C. shredded cheddar
  cheese
1 C. salsa
1 1/2 C. sour cream

Layer the lettuce, tomatoes, onions, chili, salsa, cheese and sour cream in a large bowl in that order. Serve immediately. Serves 10.

TACO DINNER SALAD

1 lb. ground beef, cooked
  and drained
1 onion, chopped
1-14 1/2 oz. can chopped
  tomatoes, undrained
1-14 oz. envelope taco
  seasoning mix
3/4 C. water
1-16 oz. can pinto beans,
  rinsed and drained

1-8 oz. pkg. pasteurized
  process cheese spread,
  cut up
Shredded lettuce
4 tortilla salad shells
Chopped tomato, shredded
  cheese, sliced ripe
  olives

In the skillet with the ground meat, add the can tomatoes, seasoning mix and 3/4 cup water. Cook for 10 more minutes over medium heat. Stir in the beans and cheese spread. Cook until cheese spread is melted. Serve in the tortilla shells and sprinkle the chopped tomato, cheese and olives. Serves 4.

TACO PASTA SALAD

1 lb. ground meat
1-1.25 oz. pkg. Ortega
  taco seasoning mix
1-16 oz. pkg. macaroni,
  cooked, rinsed and
  drained

1-16 oz. jar Ortega salsa
1 C. sliced ripe olives
3/4 C. sliced green onions

Cook the ground meat and seasoning according to package directions. Mix all together and serve. Serves 8.

DIJON BEEF TENDERLOIN SALAD

1 lb. beef tenderloin
  tips, cut into bite-size
  pieces

1 T. olive oil
10 oz. mixed salad greens
Prepared croutons

DRESSING:
1/2 C. olive oil
1/4 C. Dijon mustard
1/4 C. balsamic vinegar

1 clove garlic, crushed
1 t. sugar
1/4 t. pepper

Whisk all dressing ingredients until creamy. Set aside. Heat the olive oil in a skillet over medium-high heat until hot. Add the meat and cook for 2 to 3 minutes. Remove from the skillet. Add the greens and 1/2 cup dressing. Toss. Top with beef and croutons. Pass the remaining dressing. Serves 4.

BEEF AND PASTA SALAD

1 1/2 lbs. boneless beef
  top sirloin steak,
  grilled
4 C. uncooked tri-colored
  corkscrew pasta, cooked
1-14 oz. can artichoke
  hearts, drained and
  quartered

1 red bell pepper, cut
  into thin strips
1 C. pitted ripe olives
2 T. thinly sliced fresh
  basil
1/2 C. balsamic
  vinaigrette

Cut steak lengthwise in half, then crosswise into thin
slices. Combine all ingredients, except vinaigrette,
and mix. Pour the vinaigrette over and toss. Cover and
chill for at least 2 hours. Serves 4.

PEARS AND PORK SALAD

2 T. rice vinegar
1 t. sugar
2 T. vegetable oil
Boston lettuce, torn
6 scallions, white and
  green sliced on the
  diagonal

1/4 C. fresh cilantro
1 Asian pear, cored and
  cut into wedges
Salt and pepper to taste
12 slices roasted pork
  tenderloin

Whisk the vinegar and sugar in a large bowl. Gradually
whisk in the oil. Add the rest of the ingredients,
except pork, and toss. Place on plates with the slices
of pork on top. Serves 4.

B·L·T· SALAD

1/2 lb. bacon, cooked and
  crumbled, saving 2 T.
  drippings
1/2 C. mayonnaise
2 T. red wine vinegar
1/4 C. finely chopped
  fresh basil
4 slices French bread, cut
  into 1/2-inch pieces

1 t. salt
1 t. pepper
1 T. canola oil
1 lb. romaine lettuce,
  torn into bite-size
  pieces
1 pt. cherry tomatoes,
  quartered

In a small bowl, whisk together the reserved bacon drippings, mayonnaise, vinegar and basil. Let stand, covered, at room temperature. In a skillet over medium heat, season the bread pieces with the salt and pepper. Drizzle with the oil, continue tossing and cook over medium-low heat until golden brown. In a large bowl, mix the romaine, tomatoes, bacon and croutons. Pour the dressing over the salad and toss well.

HAWAIIAN HAM SALAD

1-3 oz. pkg. lemon gelatin
1 C. boiling water
1/2 C. heavy cream
1/2 C. mayonnaise
2 T. horseradish

1-8 1/4 oz. can crushed
  pineapple, drained
1/2 C. cottage cheese
1/2 C. pecans
1/2 C. ham, shredded

Dissolve gelatin in the boiling water. Cool slightly. Blend in cream, mayonnaise and horseradish. Fold in the remaining ingredients and chill until set.

BOW-TIE SHRIMP SALAD

1 lb. bow-tie pasta,
   cooked to al denté and
   chill
1/2 lb. large shrimp,
   deveined, tails removed
   and cooked
1 crate cherry tomatoes,
   halved

1 bunch scallions, sliced
2 C. fresh green beans,
   blanched
1 yellow bell pepper,
   seeded and sliced into
   thin rings

DRESSING:
3/4 C. mayonnaise
1/2 C. plain yogurt
1 T. dill weed
1 T. black pepper
1/2 t. kosher salt

1 T. sugar
2 T. Worcestershire sauce
1/2 C. minced fresh
   parsley
1 T. lemon juice

Mix all the salad ingredients. Mix all the dressing together. Fold into the salad mixture and chill.

I'm not a complete idiot: some parts are missing.

CONGEALED SHRIMP SALAD

1 T. unflavored gelatin
2 C. water
1-3 oz. box lemon-flavored
  gelatin
1 can condensed tomato
  soup
2-3 oz. pkg. cream cheese

1 C. chopped celery
1/2 C. chopped nuts
1/2 C. chopped bell pepper
1 C. mayonnaise
1 T. grated onion
1/2 to 1 lb. boiled
  shrimp, chopped

Soften unflavored gelatin in 1/4 cup cold water.
Dissolve with lemon-flavored gelatin in 1 1/3 cups
boiling water. Let cool. Beat in the tomato soup and
cream cheese. Fold in the rest of the ingredients.
Chill. Serve on lettuce leaves. Serves 6 to 8.

SHRIMP PASTA SALAD WITH BASIL DRESSING

8 oz. penne pasta
1 t. garlic powder
2 lbs. shrimp, cooked and
  peeled

1-10 oz. pkg. frozen peas
1 red bell pepper, chopped
1/2 C. red onion, chopped

DRESSING:
1 T. dried basil
3 cloves garlic, minced

1/3 C. olive oil
3 T. fresh lemon juice

Mix the dressing ingredients well. Mix the salad
ingredients. Pour the dressing over the salad mixture
and mix well. Serves 8.

GAZPACHO SHRIMP AND ARTICHOKE SALAD

2 T. vinegar
1 t. black peppercorns
4 medium artichokes

1 lb. shelled cooked tiny
  shrimp, peeled

DRESSING:
3 T. olive oil
1/4 C. white wine vinegar
1 garlic clove, minced
1 T. minced green onion
1 T. minced celery

1 tomato, finely chopped
1 avocado, peeled, pitted
  and diced
1 T. minced fresh cilantro

In a large pan, bring 2 quarts water, vinegar and peppercorns to boiling. Remove the outer artichoke leaves, trims stems even with bases, cut off top third of each and trim off remaining thorny leaf tips. Boil gently, covered, until bottoms are tender, 25 to 30 minutes. Drain. Pull out tiny, thorn-tipped center leaves. With a spoon, scoop out fuzzy centers. Set artichokes upright on plates, flaring leaves slightly. Mix all the dressing ingredients well. Mix with the shrimp. Spoon equally into the artichokes. Serves 4.

SHRIMP SALAD

1 lb. macaroni, cooked
1/2 C. celery, finely
  chopped
2 lbs. Shrimp, boiled and
  peeled
1 C. black olives, finely
  chopped

12 eggs, hard-cooked and
  chopped
1 C. dill pickles, chopped
1 C. onion, chopped
Mayonnaise

Add all the ingredients and add enough mayonnaise to hold it together. Serves 15.

NEW ORLEANS SHRIMP SALAD

3/4 C. cooked wild rice
1 lb. salad shrimp
3/4 t. salt
1 T. lemon juice
1 T. chopped scallion
1 T. sliced stuffed olives
1/4 C. slivered bell
  pepper

3/4 C. diced raw
  cauliflower
1/3 C. mayonnaise
1 C. finely shredded
  lettuce
2 T. French dressing

Mix all ingredients together, including lettuce. Chill and serve on lettuce leaves. Serves 4.

SHRIMP SALAD FRENCH STYLE

1 lb. fresh asparagus
3/4 lb. cooked shrimp,
  peeled and deveined
1/3 C. mayonnaise
1 T. lemon juice

6 artichoke hearts,
  drained
1 C. French dressing
2 hard-cooked eggs,
  chopped
6 sprigs fresh parsley

Cook the asparagus in boiling water until tender. Remove and cool under cold water. Hold back 6 stalks and cut the remaining asparagus into 1-inch pieces. Save 6 shrimp and chop the remainder. Mix the chopped shrimp and asparagus. Add the mayonnaise and lemon juice. In a separate bowl, marinate the artichoke hearts in 1 cup French dressing. Place the chopped shrimp and asparagus in a shallow bowl. Add the eggs and parsley on top. Arrange around this, the asparagus spears, whole shrimp and artichoke hearts.

SHRIMP AND MACARONI SALAD

DRESSING:

1 C. light mayonnaise
1 t. seasoned salt
1/2 t. celery seed

1 t. salt
1/2 t. pepper
2 T. brown spicy mustard

SALAD:

3 ribs celery, chopped
3 tomatoes, diced
1 bunch green onions,
  chopped

1 lb. cooked shrimp,
  peeled
1-16 oz. shell macaroni,
  cooked

Combine all the dressing ingredients. Place the salad ingredients in a bowl and toss with the dressing. Mix well. Refrigerate 2 hours before serving.

SALMON PASTA SALAD

1 lb. fresh salmon fillet
1-8 oz. pkg. spiral pasta
1/3 C. mayonnaise
3/4 C. nonfat plain yogurt
1/2 t. sugar

2 t. dried dill weed
1/2 t. white pepper
1 C. celery, diced
1-14 oz. can hearts of
    palm, drained and sliced

Preheat the oven to 325 degrees F. Place the salmon in a shallow baking dish coated with nonstick cooking spray and bake for about 15 minutes, or until done. Set aside to cool. Cook the pasta according to package directions, omitting any oil and salt. Drain, rinse and set aside. Mix the mayonnaise, yogurt, sugar, dill weed and pepper. Set aside. In a large bowl, mix the celery, hearts of palm, pasta and dressing. Remove the skin from the salmon and flake into chunks. Add to the pasta mixture, tossing gently. Chill. Serves 4.

SALMON SALAD

1-8 oz. can red sockeye
  salmon, drained
1/2 C. orange juice
1/4 C. lemon juice
1 green bell pepper,
  chopped

1 cucumber, chopped
1 tomato, chopped
1/2 red onion, minced
3 T. green onions, minced
4 lettuce leaves
4 lime wedges

Crush the salmon bones and break salmon into bite-size pieces. Mix the orange and lemon juice and pour over the salmon. Set aside. Combine the green pepper, cucumber, tomato and onions. Add 1/3 of the vegetable mixture to the salmon mixture. Marinate this and refrigerate for 2 to 3 hours.

To serve, arrange salmon salad on lettuce leaf. Place the reserved vegetables over the salmon. Serve with lime wedges. Serves 4.

CRABMEAT SALAD

1-16 oz. pkg. imitation
  crabmeat, shredded into
  bite-sized pieces
3/4 C. mayonnaise

3 stalks celery, chopped
5 T. finely chopped onion
1 carrot, shredded

Combine all and chill for 1 hour before serving. Serves 4.

CRAB SALAD IN PINEAPPLE SHELLS

2-6 oz. pkg. frozen Alaska
  King crab, thawed and
  drained
3 C. cold cooked rice
1 C. coarsely chopped ripe
  olives
1/2 C. diced celery

1/2 C. chopped parsley
1/3 C. mayonnaise
3 T. bottled creamy French
  dressing
1 t. curry powder
1 large pineapple

Cut pineapple in half lengthwise. Scoop out the pineapple, leaving 1/2-inch-thick shells. Cover and refrigerate. Cut the pineapple that was scooped out into chunks. In a large bowl, toss all ingredients, cover and refrigerate until ready to serve. Place the salad in the pineapple shells. Serves 6.

Everyone has a photographic memory. Some just don't have film.

LOBSTER SALAD

1/2 C. mayonnaise
6 T. puréed spinach
Salt to taste
Freshly ground black
  pepper
Cayenne pepper
Lemon juice
1 lobster, cooked in court
  bouillon

1/2 t. cucumber, diced
2 hard-cooked eggs, diced
3 ripe avocados, diced
Juice of 2 lemons
Minced tarragon
Minced chives
Minced parsley

Combine the mayonnaise and spinach. Season to taste
with the salt, peppers and a little lemon juice. Pass
through a fine sieve. Dice lobster meat. Marinate the
avocados in the lemon juice. Mix the meat, drained
avocados, cucumber and eggs. Add the green sauce and
toss. Chill. Just before serving, add the minced
tarragon, chives and parsley on top. Serves 6.

MEDITERRANEAN TUNA SALAD

1 can tuna, packed in
  water
1 T. chopped basil
1 C. cooked black beans,
  rinsed and drained
1/2 C. diced red onion
1 stalk celery, finely
  diced

1 1/2 t. lemon juice
1 t. grated lemon peel
1 1/2 T. olive oil
1/2 t. coarsely ground
  black pepper
2 T. chopped green olives

Mix all the ingredients. Serves 2.

LOUISIANA TUNA SALAD

1-6 1/2 can tuna, drained
3 hard-cooked eggs,
  chopped
2 T. mayonnaise

2 T. dill relish
1 t. Louisiana hot sauce
2 T. Dijon mustard

Mix all the ingredients, cover and chill. If too dry,
add more mayonnaise. Serves 8.

CRUNCHY TUNA SALAD

1-6 1/2 oz. can solid
  white tuna packed in
  water, drained and flaked
1-8 oz. can water
  chestnuts, drained and
  chopped
1 C. celery, chopped

1/2 C. carrots, shredded
1/4 C. green onions,
  sliced
1/4 C. mayonnaise
1 T. Dijon mustard
1 t. soy sauce
1/4 t. pepper

Mix all the ingredients and chill. Serves 2.

I smile because I have no idea what's going on.

TUNA SALAD AND FETTUCCINE

2-7 oz. cans tuna in oil
1/4 C. olive oil
1 large clove garlic,
  minced
4 oz. fresh mushrooms,
  chopped
1 C. broccoli florets
1 zucchini, diced

1 red bell pepper, seeded
  and chopped
2 T. minced fresh basil
8 oz. fettuccine
1/2 t. black pepper
4 oz. Swiss cheese,
  shredded
Italian salad dressing

Drain the oil from the tuna and place the oil in a large skillet. Place the tuna in a large bowl and separate into chunks. Set aside. Add the olive oil to the skillet and heat. Add the garlic, mushrooms, broccoli, zucchini and bell pepper. Cook over medium-low heat, stirring occasionally until vegetables are tender, about 5 minutes. Add the basil and stir a few times and remove from the heat. Let cool. Cook the fettuccine according to the package. Drain well. Add the noodles, vegetables and tuna together. Add the pepper and lemon juice. Toss. Cover and refrigerate for at least 30 minutes. Before serving, arrange on lettuce leaves and serve with the Italian dressing. Serves 4.

Make it idiot-proof, and someone will make a better idiot.

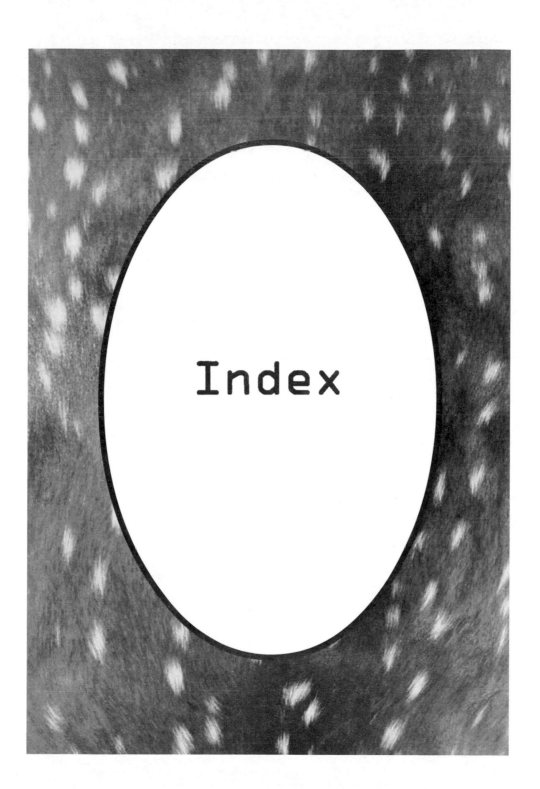

Index

SOUPS

Baked Potato Soup 21
Barley Beef Soup 1
Basil Veggie Soup 10
Beefy Tortilla Soup 1
Black Bean and Salsa Soup 10
Broccoli Cheese Soup 17
Broccoli Soup 18
Chicken Salsa Soup 6
Chicken Taco Soup 5
Corn Chowder 20
Crab Soup 8
Crab Soup 9
Cream of Asparagus Soup 18
Cream of Mushroom Soup 19
Cream of Spinach Soup 14
Egg Drop Soup 14
Eight-Can Soup 2
Fast Crab Bisque 8
Hash Brown Potato Soup 21
Lobster Bisque 7
Pasta Fagioli 13
Quick Vegetable Soup .9
Santa Fe Squash Soup 16
Shrimp and Artichoke Soup 7
Six-Can Chicken Tortilla Soup 6
Split Pea Soup 13
Squash Soup 15
Squash Soup II 15
Sweet Potato Soup 22
Tex-Mex Turkey Soup 4
Three-Bean Soup 11
Tortellini, White Bean and Spinach Soup 12
Tuscany Tomato Soup 20
Turkey and Barley Soup 3
Wild Rice and Mushroom Soup 19

SALAD DRESSINGS

PASTA SALADS

FRUIT SALADS

MEAT AND SEAFOOD SALADS

Notes

THE COOKBOOK CO.

ANY BITCH CAN COOK

ANY BITCH CAN PARTY

ANY BITCH CAN DRINK

SUGAR BITCHES

ANY BITCH CAN FAKE IT

ANY BITCH CAN SALSA

MERRY BITCHIN HOLIDAYS

EAT BITCH & WINE

ANY QUEEN CAN DECORATE

ANY BITCH CAN HEAT IT UP

BITCHIN & GRILLIN

www.anybitchcookbooks.com